LIVING
on the
EDGE

LIVING
on the
EDGE

DREAMS, DETOURS, *and* DESTINY

DR. SHANON EATON

XULON PRESS

Xulon Press
2301 Lucien Way #415
Maitland, FL 32751
407.339.4217
www.xulonpress.com

Unless otherwise indicated, Scriptures marked (NASB) are taken from the New American Standard Bible, Copyright © 1960, 1962, 1963, 1968, 1971, 1972, 1973, 1975, 1977, 1995 by The Lockman Foundation.

Scriptures marked (NLT) are taken from the Holy Bible, New Living Translation, copyright © 1996, 2004, 2007, 2013, 2015 by Tyndale House Foundation. Used by permission of Tyndale House Publishers Inc., Carol Stream, Illinois 60188. All rights reserved.

Scriptures marked (NIV) are taken from the Holy Bible, New International Version®, NIV® Copyright ©1973, 1978, 1984, 2011 by Biblica, Inc.® Used by permission. All rights reserved worldwide.

Scriptures marked (NKJV) are taken from the New King James Version®. Copyright © 1982 by Thomas Nelson. Used by permission. All rights reserved.

Scriptures marked (ESV) are taken from The Holy Bible, English Standard Version. ESV® Text Edition: 2016. Copyright © 2001 by Crossway Bibles, a publishing ministry of Good News Publishers.

Scriptures marked (KJV) are taken from the King James Version (KJV) Public Domain.

Printed in the United States of America

Paperback ISBN-13: 978-1-6628-1742-7
Ebook ISBN-13: 978-1-6628-1743-4

DEDICATION

This Book is Dedicated to my loving and devoted wife Jessica Eaton. It is your care, compassion, daily and constant encouragement, and devotion that has made this work possible.

ACKNOWLEDGMENTS

There are many people who have been great sources of encouragement for me and the ministry to which God has called me. I am grateful to my parents Bishop Thomas Eaton and Jeannie Eaton for setting the example for me in faithfulness and commitment. I would not be where I am without the encouragement and belief of Pastors Norm and Dina Dubois. Your kindness and willingness to always be a voice of faith and reason in my life is a treasure that I will always value. I will never for get you being one of the first to truly believe in me and all that God has chosen to do in my life. Pastors Eugene and Laura Smith, you are absolutely remarkable and I am truly grateful for your willingness to constantly encourage me to "keep fighting the good fight" and to never quit. Your faith and dedication have been truly great examples as we have sought to walk out the plan of God for our lives. Pastors Joe and Terri Manno, you are true examples of commitment to hearing from God and obeying what He says. Pastors Guinn and Karen Shingleton, your words and prayers on an ongoing basis have been a great blessing that has help to keep my fire for the things of God burning. Bishop Vaughn McLaughlin, you have caused me to think deeply and strongly about remaining committed to the Gospel of Jesus Christ and to the calling of God upon my life. Your encouragement and faithfulness in helping pastors and leaders is a true gem and rarity in the Kingdom. Pastors Jimmy and Lydia Nimon, you have been there since the beginning of the journey and you have been one of the great faith builders in my life. I'm truly honored to call you not only friends, but family. Pastor Tim & Krystal Staier, you have always been there from day one and you have been a true source of strength and encouragement in my life from day one. Pastors Adam and Rebecca Peterson, words cannot describe all you have done to help me in walking out the pastoral call on my life. Pastors Darryl and Kara Bellar, you have been true friends. Your courageous leadership have been a great blessing to my life and a true encouragement in the ministry. Pastor Corey Williams, I appreciate your consistency in leading and your authentic encouragement to me. I most also thank two amazing leaders and brothers in Pastor Justin Gaston and Pastor T.L. Gainer. You both have been a great source of faith building and encouragement. A word of appreciation must Dr. Larry Keefauver and the editing team for helping to bring this work to fruition. Thank you for your handwork and dedication.

ENDORSMENTS

Shanon Eaton is great listener, learner, and leader. A very rare combination! If Pastor Shanon is talking, it is because he has something to say. You'll will always leave encouraged and strengthened by his wisdom and blessed by his humility. Most importantly, Shanon is a servant leader. He always has your best interest at heart.

This book is a must read for those who are serious about making a difference in this life. Pastor Shanon will mentor you through this book on staying the course. You will receive powerful principles and clear applications. Get ready to be challenged and encouraged at the same time. Whether you are a new believer or a seasoned believer you will find the principles in this book will refresh you and keep you on track. If you want to finish strong, read this book!
Norm Dubois, Senior Pastor East Coast Believers Church, Oviedo, FL

"Over the years I've had the privilege of watching Dr. Shanon Eaton and his wife, Jessica, walk out the life giving principals from this book. From his days as high school Vice Principal, to growing his family and stepping out in faith to plant Life City Church, Shanon and Jessica have modeled what it means to live a life of, "Living on the Edge."
Eugene Smith, Senior Pastor, City Church, Sanford FL

When I have a big decision to make in life or ministry, Shanon Eaton is one of the first people I go to for guidance. His God-given ability to distill biblical wisdom into action steps is a gift from God. Living on the edge is your starting point to living out the Christian life.
Darryl E Bellar, Senior Pastor The Journey Church, Fernadina Beach, FL

Destiny is the idea that your life is going somewhere. In this book, Dr. Shanon Eaton takes us on that journey exposing us to important lessons, that if grasped, help us lay hold of that for which Christ has laid hold of us. Written with devotional quality, this book has within it the guideposts of God's principles that the prayerful disciple of God will want for life.
Jimmy Nimon, Senior Pastor Lifeway Church, Lebanon, PA

From the first time we met, I knew that God's hand was on Shanon Eaton and his family. In the years since, I've seen why: he is one of the most authentically good people I've met–and he's brilliant on top of that! His new book, *Living on the Edge*, is about dreaming and DOING all that God has put in your heart, and I've watched Shanon do just that. As you read through the ups and downs of believing for the impossible, I know you'll be encouraged to discover and develop the God-given dream in you.
Tim Staier, Senior Pastor Elevate Life Church, Jacksonville, Fl

Dr. Shanon Eaton is one of the most genuine and compassionate people I've ever met. His appetite to learn and grow is what makes him an incredible leader. His humility and encouragement is what makes people want to follow him.
Adam Peterson, Senior Pastor, Rise Church, Jacksonville, FL

Shanon Eaton is one of the most brilliant people I've ever met. His words are edifying and inspiring. He's a breath of fresh air to a faith community that is in dire need of integrative leaders. I'm honored to know Shannon and beautiful family. I'm glad he's writing this book, the body of Christ will benefit from this. *Justin Gaston, Lead Pastor, Presence Church, Perry GA*

Pastor Shanon is by far one of the most intentional teachers of the gospel that I know. He has an unwavering compassion of not only impacting lives but helping them discover their purpose so that they are able to live out what God has destined for them. I am truly blessed to call him a friend and a brother. *T.L. Gainer, Senior Pastor, Refreshing Worship Christian Church, Fayetteville, GA*

TABLE OF CONTENTS

Introduction

LIVING ON THE EDGE OF DESTINY

L ife is full of twists and turns. Sometimes, we feel as though we know where we are going. Other times, we feel as though we do not. Often, it seems as though we have a grip on our ultimate purpose and destiny. Yet other times, it is almost as if we are traveling aimlessly on a never-ending road to nowhere.

Perhaps you have felt this way. Maybe you have had moments in your life in which everything seemed so clear. It seemed as if you had no shortage of passion and enthusiasm for the direction your life was taking. Yet, at other times you may have had that draining feeling of a life void of energy, instruction, direction, and destiny. This is the roller coaster journey of the person who constantly lives on the edge of destiny.

This book is intended to be an encouragement to those of you who have experienced the see-saw of both certainty and skepticism regarding the purpose and plan God has for your life. It is intended to show you that when you pursue the dream and the vision that God has for you, it may take longer than you think as life leads you down a path that you didn't imagine. You might be thinking that this doesn't sound very encouraging. The reality is that it is extremely encouraging because God's path for us is always perfect. God's ways are always best.

God has not promised that everything would be comfortable, but He does convey that He is completely faithful, totally reliable, and always trustworthy.

Throughout the pages of this book, we will explore the life of one of the Bible's most polarizing figures. His name is Joseph, son of Jacob. I believe we can all find ourselves somewhere in the life experiences of this amazing man who was used so mightily by God. Joseph's life embodies the truth that when God has a plan, vision, or dream for our lives it will certainly come to pass. The life of Joseph teaches us that God does not sit at the mercy of temporary circumstances.

We can learn from the life of Joseph that no matter how the story of our life appears to have been written, God always writes the final chapter.

The other thing we will be able to clearly observe from Joseph's life and be able to apply to our own life is that things seldom go as we actually expect them to go. This important to understand since we often feel like we know what God will do in our lives, but become distracted and discouraged by the path that it may take for us to get there. When we realize this, we can continue to hold on to the vision, dream, purposes, plans, and promises of God even when what we see does not look anything like what He said.

GOD'S PRINCIPLES

God always works things out for His greatest glory and our highest good. God does not think and act as we do or would.

These two important principles are important for us to remember as we begin this journey through Joseph's life. First, **God always works things out for His greatest glory and our highest good.** Paul expresses in Romans 8:28, "And we know that God causes all things to work together for good to those who love

God, to those who are called according to His purpose" (NASB). This should bring us great comfort. As we will see through the life of Joseph, many of the individual circumstances of our lives may not be good, God is a master craftsman and is able to weave everything perfectly together for our good and for His glory.

The second principle may appear overly simple, yet it is anything but easy to grasp. As Isaiah 55:8-9 conveys to us, **God does not think and act as we do or would.** "For My thoughts are not your thoughts, Nor are your ways My ways," declares the Lord. For as the heavens are higher than the earth, So are My ways higher than your ways And My thoughts than your thoughts" (NASB). In short, it is easy for us to agree with God on His vision for our lives, yet it can be much more difficult to surrender to His method or path for how He chooses to accomplish His plan in our lives.

Fulfilling the purpose of God in our lives will teach us a healthy level of humility and surrender. Ultimately, humility and surrender will help us to realize God knows better than we do. If we are honest, most of us would choose the path of least resistance to get to any place that we would attempt to go. Throughout the pages of scripture, we can see that God's method is almost always the direct opposite.

As we begin our journey, open your minds and hearts to the path of faithfulness and surrender. It is always the best way. Pray and ask God to reawaken the dreams that you may have buried in the grave of uncertainty, fear, doubt, and discouragement. Be reminded that because you have life and you have breath, you have a purpose. You can be assured of the fulfillment of God's purpose and vision for your life because it comes from Him. As you read the pages of this book, you will be challenged to build the endurance and perseverance to refuse to give up.

The foundation of faith and belief in the manifestation of God's plan is the power, presence, and faithfulness of God. We must have complete faith in God's ability to fulfill His plan for our lives.

Let faith arise and believe the words recorded in Psalm 138:8, "The Lord will work out his plans for my life— for your faithful love, O Lord, endures forever. Don't abandon me, for you made me" (NLT). The reason we can have confidence is because we do not focus on our own ability, glory, or ambition, but on the character and faithfulness of God to carry out what He has promised.

Let's prepare to receive the truths of God's Word through the life of Joseph by beginning with prayer. Pray the prayer below out loud individually, with your family, or silently as you trust God to work in your life.

Dear Heavenly Father, we come to You with expectation and dedication. We believe that You truly do have a plan, a purpose, and a vision for our lives. We ask You to remove from us anything that would keep us from clearly seeing Your vision and dream for our lives. We confess that regardless of any circumstance or struggle we may personally be experiencing, that You are still faithful. Thank You for loving us enough to carry us along the best path for our lives. Thank You for maturing us and growing us through every test so that the manifestation of Your intended destiny for our lives would bring You glory and cause others to know You. We humble ourselves and surrender to Your way even though we may often not understand it. As we read through each chapter, give us eyes that see, ears that hear, and a heart that will believe, receive, and obey every principle You reveal to us. We pray these things humbly and expectantly believing, in Jesus' name, Amen.

REVIEW GOD'S PRINCIPLES

At the end of each chapter, we will remind you of the important principles God has revealed to us in that chapter.

God always works things out for His greatest glory and our highest good.

God does not think and act as we do or would.

Reflect on how these principles encourage you on your personal journey living on the edge of destiny.

Chapter 1
IT BEGINS WITH A DREAM

We begin our journey at what will prove to be the first critical stage of Joseph's life. As we will explore Joseph's life throughout this book, we will see what it looks like to have a dream and see it fulfilled. We will also discover there are many aspects of life we may be tempted to overlook at the time, but that play a relevant part in getting us to our destiny. Walking in destiny and purpose often feels great and generates enthusiasm and excitement until we realize that the journey starts becoming anything but ideal.

As we look at the beginning of Joseph's destiny journey, we can lift several helpful principles from both a spiritual and a practical standpoint. It all begins with a dream he had as a teenager.

Favor Is...

The Vine's Dictionary defines favor as "the position one enjoys before a superior who is favorably disposed toward him; to be pleased with, delighted with, goodwill, acceptance."[1]

GOD'S PRINCIPLES

Favor is not always comfortable.
Favor does not come without tests and challenges.

---

[1] Vine's Complete Expository of Old and New Testament Words, ©1984, 1996, Thomas Nelson, Inc., Nashville, TN.

The first two principles we can observe from the life of Joseph is that **favor is not always comfortable.** What we can initially see here and will eventually see throughout Joseph's life is that **favor does not come without tests and challenges.**

> *Now Jacob lived in the land where his father had sojourned, in the land of Canaan. These are the records of the generations of Jacob. Joseph, when **seventeen years of age**, was pasturing the flock with his brothers while he was still a youth, along with the sons of Bilhah and the sons of Zilpah, his father's wives. And Joseph brought back a bad report about them to their father. Now **Israel loved Joseph more than all his sons**, because he was the son of his old age; and he made him a varicolored tunic. **His brothers saw that their father loved him more than all his brothers; and so they hated him and could not speak to him on friendly terms**.* (Genesis 37:1-4 NASB emphasis added)

One of the most amazing things about the Bible is that it gives us the nitty-gritty at times. It does not consider certain things as insignificant details. For example, the Bible begins documenting Joseph's amazing destiny journey telling us Joseph was a teenager and apparently a bit of a snitch or a tattletale. You can imagine this likely didn't do much good for family morale and relational stability with his brothers. Apparently, Joseph had no problem working with them and then sharing all of their shortcomings with their father at the same time. While we don't know the complete scope of his brothers' behaviors, we can see that Joseph didn't necessarily appear to be concerned with having favor with them.

However, we also learn that Joseph was his father's favorite son. In considering current parenting challenges, most parents would say they love all of their children equally, but differently. This apparently was not the case at all in regard to Israel and Joseph. We find that Israel made it obvious through his actions that Joseph was his favorite. However, **favor can bring both blessings and challenges.**

Imagine being Joseph and being showered with the love of your father on a regular basis. We aren't talking about a little extra dessert or escaping discipline. We are talking about visible evidence showing extreme favor with no attempt to hide it from those who are watching. The only solid indication we are given from the scriptures above regarding the reason Joseph received this level of favor from his father was that he was born when his father was old. Joseph was so loved by his father that Israel made Joseph what is commonly referred to as a "coat of many colors."[2] To make this plain, his father made something visibly extravagant for him that he did not make for his other sons.

GOD'S PRINCIPLES

**Favor can bring both blessings and challenges.
Favor may have unintended,
unanticipated, and unimagined consequences.
Favor not only brings great blessing, it also comes with a
high price tag.**

In Joseph's case, his father's favor caused his brothers to both hate him and be jealous of him. In fact, his brothers not only hated him and were jealous of him, but they also had so much disdain for him that they found it literally impossible to speak to him on friendly terms.

It is with this foundation that we find Joseph experiencing his first recorded dream.

Destiny Begins with a Dream

Then Joseph had a dream, and when he told it to his brothers, they hated him even more. He said to them, "Please listen to this dream which I have had; for behold,

---

[2] In the simplest sense, Joseph's coat of many colors symbolized favor. It was a garment given to Joseph by his father Jacob. It wasn't a work garment like his brothers would wear, rather an elaborate work of art that was made to stand out. It spoke of nobility, not hard work. (crosswalk.com)

> *we were binding sheaves in the field, and lo, my sheaf*
> *rose up and also stood erect; and behold, your sheaves*
> *gathered around and bowed down to my sheaf." Then his*
> *brothers said to him, "Are you actually going to reign*
> *over us? Or are you really going to rule over us?" So* **they**
> **hated him even more for his dreams and for his words**.
> (Genesis 37:5-8 NASB emphasis added)

A dream may be defined as a series of images, thoughts, and feelings occurring while one is asleep.[3] We cannot be fully sure why Joseph chose to share this dream with brothers who didn't even like him. Maybe he shared it because he hoped it would draw them closer together and improve their relationship. We could also speculate he shared it to rub the contents of the dream in their faces. We only know when he shared his dream, it caused his brothers to hate him even more than they already did. Just because one has a dream, it does not mean that they have developed the maturity to handle the dream.

So, why would his brothers choose to listen to a dream from a brother they hated so much? John H. Walton gives some insight as to why his brothers may have elected to listen to this dream. He suggests, "Dreams in the ancient world were considered derived from the divine realm and were thus taken seriously."[4]

People paid attention to dreams because they were believed to be from God. As such, this dream would be exciting to Joseph, but disheartening to his jealous brothers. In essence, Joseph was relaying to them a dream that indicated he would be more significant than they were. The other thing that is important to note is that his brothers also grasped an immediate interpretation of what they thought the dream might mean.

Before we lay out some principles of Joseph's experience with conveying his dreams, we need to look at his second dream.

---

[3]   Merriam-Webster's Collegiate Dictionary, ©2009

[4]   John H. Walton, Genesis: *The New Application Commentary*. Zondervan. p.663 (Grand Rapids MI, 2001)

Now he had still another dream, and related it to his brothers, and said, "Lo, I have had still another dream; and behold, the sun and the moon and eleven stars were bowing down to me." He related it to his father and to his brothers; and his father rebuked him and said to him, "What is this dream that you have had? Shall I and your mother and your brothers actually come to bow ourselves down before you to the ground?" His brothers were jealous of him, but his father kept the saying in mind. (Genesis 37:9-11 NASB)

We can see Joseph's second dream drawing a response from both his father and his brothers. The dream actually brought a rebuke from the father who favored him and jealousy from the brothers who hated him.

In looking at the experience of Joseph's dreams, there are several more important principles. It should be noted that some of these principles will be spiritual while others will be practical.

GOD'S PRINCIPLES

The dream that we believe should draw or attract admiration, sometimes causes hatred, envy, and jealousy.

**We often do not remotely understand
or grasp the scope of our dream.**

In short, just because God gives us a dream does not mean that everyone is obligated to believe in that dream. We must often be reminded that God gave the dream to us and not necessarily to share with others.

The next thing that it is crucial to understand is though we may be given a dream or a vision from God about our lives, **we often do not remotely understand or grasp the scope of that dream**. This is truly a point that reminds us God is bigger than we are and thinks much differently than we do. He is often showing us things with wide-ranging implications and long-term plans. We often think in terms of the immediate, the perceived urgent, and the right now. Being human, we tend to always be slightly short-sighted.

GOD'S PRINCIPLES

When we are given a dream or vision from God, we must sometimes practice the strategy of silence.

Friction may often be caused by our dreams *and* our words.

The next principle of how we handle dreams must be briefly looked at from both a practical and a spiritual standpoint. This is the place in which we must trust the sovereignty of God and ask for the wisdom of God. **When we are given a dream or vision from God, we must sometimes practice the strategy of silence.** People cannot hate you for a dream that they don't know about.

It is one thing for God to show us something. It is quite another thing to understand whether it is wise to share what we have been shown. The beautiful thing about this is that it must be balanced with the spiritual understanding that God is firmly in control. When we confidently understand that God is in control, we can see that **friction may often be caused by our dreams *and* our words**. This is why it is crucial to have both the wisdom of God and the confidence in His complete control.

As you will discover, the conveying of Joseph's initial dreams sets in motion a less than ideal journey to God's intended destination for his life. The journey that Joseph travels in his life provides evidence and proof to us that God will use the circumstances of our lives to grow us, mature us, inspire those around us, and ultimately, show Himself glorious and mighty through our lives.

In the next chapter, we will take a brief but necessary detour. We will look at the concept of tests and trials in the life of those who belong to God. While tests and trials are often unpleasant, they are a necessary step to developing the character needful to fully carry out the dream and vision God has for our lives.

Father, help us to hold on to the dream and the vision that You have for our lives. Make Your will so clear to us that our response is surrender. Help us to understand any practical strategic aspect of fulfilling Your vision for our lives. Give us the wisdom to know when to speak and when to be silent. Help us to be mindful and properly recognize the divine connections that You have placed in our lives to further Your purpose. We ask that You guide us to daily develop every character trait necessary to see You glorified and honored through our lives, in Jesus' name, Amen.

REVIEW GOD'S PRINCIPLES

Here are the important principles God has revealed to us in that chapter.

+ **Favor is not always comfortable. favor does not come without tests and challenges.**

+ **Favor can bring both blessings and challenges.**

+ **Favor may have unintended, unanticipated, and unimagined consequences.**

+ **Favor not only brings great blessing, but it comes with a high price tag.**

+ **The dream that we believe should draw or attract admiration sometimes causes hatred, envy, and jealousy.**

+ **We often do not remotely understand or grasp the scope of our dream.**

+ **When we are given a dream or vision from God, we must sometimes practice the strategy of silence.**

+ **Friction may often be caused by our dreams *and* our words.**

Reflect on how these principles encourage you on your personal journey living on the edge of destiny and how to correctly handle the dreams given to you by God.

Chapter 2
IT'S ONLY A TEST, OR IS IT?

In exploring the life of Joseph, one cannot look at it in any meaningful way without taking a slight detour. Joseph's life really cannot be properly understood apart from dealing with the concept of testing. My hope in doing this is to provide a lens by which we can properly filter the different experiences Joseph went through. By understanding the concept of testing, we will begin to see the benefit in the trials we may face along the way. As with Joseph's life, **every major crossroads we may come to in life accomplishes something in us where we are and prepares us for next the stage of our life.**

> *"He sent a man before them, Joseph, who was sold as a slave. They afflicted his feet with fetters, He himself was laid in irons; Until the time that his **word** came to pass, The **word** of the Lord tested him."* (Psalm 105:18-19 NASB emphasis added)

One of the unique aspects of this passage of scripture is that is it uses the word "word" twice. With that said the word does not have the same meaning each time it is used. The first time "word" occurs in this passage it is referring to *a message, communication, or saying*. The second time "word" is used it means *commandment*. Understanding this is crucial to understanding a major principle that we can glean from Joseph's life. We can summarize the meaning of the verses this way. Until the complete manifestation

9

of Joseph's dream came into fulfillment, his character was consistently tested by the Word and ways of God.

GOD'S PRINCIPLES

Every major crossroads we may come to in life accomplishes something in us and prepares us for next the stage of our life.

If we are going to walk in the vision and dream God has for our life, we will have to pass various stages of testing.

Testing produces a lasting benefit in our lives. Few would say that testing feels good or comfortable. Even fewer might say that they would voluntarily seek to be tested.

Faith that has not been tested is faith that cannot be trusted.

The good news is, that as we walk with God and seek to live out His plan and purpose for our lives, we don't have to find testing. Testing will find us.

Throughout the rest of this chapter, we will look at what the Bible reveals about testing and how the principles of testing should actually bring us comfort in our Christian experience. This will also assist us in properly framing the life of Joseph and its application to our own lives.

> *Consider it all joy, my brethren, when you encounter various trials, knowing that the testing of your faith produces endurance. And let endurance have its perfect result, so that you may be perfect and complete, lacking in nothing.* (James 1:2-4 NASB emphasis added)

James instructs us to take a posture and attitude of joy when we experience tests and trials. This most certainly appears to be counterintuitive. Most of us don't go around doing cartwheels and backflips when we go through tough times. What is important to note is that we are given the reason that we are supposed to have this kind of attitude. Simply put, **our tests produce the character trait of endurance in our lives**. "Endurance" is the ability to bear up under difficult circumstances. Endurance can also be called staying power and the ability to last.

If we are to fulfill the vision, dream, and mandate God has for our lives, we must be able to stick with it and not give up when things get difficult.

Testing Is Not Punishment

The next important aspect of testing to understand is it does **not** come because we have done something wrong.

> *The Lord tests the righteous and the wicked, and the one who loves violence His soul hates.* (Psalm 11:5 NASB emphasis added)

One of the most potentially discouraging aspects of testing is believing that it is always the result of something we have done wrong. More often than not, the Bible tends to show us that when we are in right standing with God, He continues to allow testing to perfect and mature us.

GOD'S PRINCIPLES

One of the biggest truths we can learn is God does indeed test us.

God has promised a blessing to those who endure and persevere during trials.

> *Blessed is **a man who perseveres under trial**; for once he has been approved, he **will receive the crown of life** which the Lord has promised to those who love Him.* (James 1:12 NASB emphasis added)

God has promised a blessing to those who endure and per-severe during trials. Most of us can agree that at times we have experienced such severe testing that we wanted to quit and give up. Quite frankly, some of the things that we experience in our lives can cause us to abandon the calling and assignment that God has upon our lives.

As we will see in the coming chapters, the life of Joseph shows us that there will be seasons and periods in our lives in which what we see looks very little if at all like what God has promised.

One of the key concepts and principles that we can learn during seasons of testing is **we must believe what God said regardless of the present circumstances.**

The voice and promises of God must always speak louder then the fear produced by our struggles.

As we have already seen, testing produces endurance and per-severance in our lives. We are also aware of the truth that testing does come into our lives because we have done something wrong. With that said, we must explore probably the most important prin-ciple of testing.

Moses said to the people, "Do not be afraid; for God has come in order to test you, and in order that the fear of Him may remain with you, so that you may not sin." (Exodus 20:20 NASB emphasis added)

According to this passage, it is clear that **a primary purpose and aim in God testing us is so that we will reverence Him, take His commands seriously, and avoid sin at any cost.**

It is often through the tests and the trials of life that we learn the importance of clinging to God's Word, God's commands, and God's promises. The very things that the enemy wants us to abandon during our tests are often the very things that God wants us to mature, grow, and develop in during the trial.

GOD'S PRINCIPLES

**We must believe what God said
regardless of the present circumstances.**

**A primary purpose and aim in God testing us
is so that we will reverence Him, take His commands
seriously, and avoid sin at any cost.**

**Our test may actually seem like a surprise to us,
but it is never a surprise to God.**

As we look at testing, we cannot explore this without understanding one crucial point. Testing is not strange or foreign to the experience of the child of God.

Beloved, do not be surprised at the fiery ordeal among you, which comes upon you for your testing, as though some strange things were happening to you. (1 Peter 4:12 NASB)

This is a powerful verse. As you read it, you can probably think of some very difficult tests and struggles you have experienced in your life. You may even be going through some right now. The truth we can glean is even though the test may difficult, it is not strange. Much modern thinking in Christianity and the church might lead us to believe that testing should not and could not ever be a part of our experience as believers. The Bible conveys something much different. This principle could be summed up this way. As believers, we may experience very challenging tests. They may be hard, but they should not be surprising. We can find comfort and solace in knowing that if God brings us to it, He will also bring us through it.

GOD'S PRINCIPLES

We should value testing because testing has eternal worth.

**Testing teaches us to rejoice in the Lord
regardless of what we are going through.**

Testing often proves the genuineness of our faith.

This brings us to the final principle of testing that we will explore in this chapter. **We should value testing because testing has eternal worth.**

> *In this, you greatly rejoice, even though now for a little while, if necessary, you have been distressed by various trials, so that the proof of your faith, being more precious than gold which is perishable, even though tested by fire, may be found to result in praise and glory and honor at the revelation of Jesus Christ.* (1 Peter 1:6-7 NASB)

When we look at the passage above, we can make several observations that will help us in our walk with the Lord as well as help us to have to proper sense through which we can understand the life of Joseph. **Testing teaches us to rejoice in the Lord regardless of what we are going through.**

It is important to note that God's Word does not ignore the intensity of our test, but reminds us of the proper posture to take during tests and the reason why we should take that posture. Simply put, **testing often proves the genuineness of our faith.** The genuineness of our faith that is revealed by enduring tests will prove to be of lasting worth and value to us. More important than that, God will be glorified through our experience.

As we include this chapter, I want to challenge you not to despise your tests but to embrace them. Notice I did not say to enjoy them. While the various tests and struggles that we may experience in our lives may not make us happy, if we stick it out, they will make us both fruitful and productive in the fulfillment of all God desires to do in our lives.

Prayer

Father, in the name of Jesus, grant me the strength to both embrace and endure the various tests I may experience in my life. I often do not know when or how tests will show up in my life. In these moments, help me to remain focused on You, Your Word, and Your promises. Help me to daily embrace Your faithfulness, love, and care for me regardless of what I may experience. Produce in me everything You need to produce in order to get the glory out of my life. Thank You for remaining true to Your promises and for using every means at Your disposal to help me to become fully mature and ready to fulfill the mandate You have for my life.

REVIEW GOD'S PRINCIPLES

Here are the important principles God has revealed to us in that chapter.

✦ **Every major crossroads we may come to in life accomplishes something in us and prepares us for next the stage of our life.**

✦ **If we are going to walk in the vision and dream God has for our life, we will have to pass various stages of testing.**

✦ **God has promised a blessing to those who endure and persevere during trials.**

✦ **One of the biggest truths we can learn is God does indeed test us.**

✦ **A primary purpose and aim in God testing us is so that we will reverence Him, take His commands seriously, and avoid sin at any cost.**

✦ **We must believe what God said regardless of the present circumstances.**

✦ **Testing teaches us to rejoice in the Lord regardless of what we are going through.**

✦ **Testing often proves the genuineness of our faith.**

Reflect on how these principles encourage you on your personal journey living on the edge of destiny and how to correctly handle the tests and trials given to you by God.

Chapter 3

VISION: I CAN SEE CLEARLY NOW, BUT CAN I?

B efore we continue to dive into the life of Joseph, I want to address a critical part of walking in the dream that God has for our lives. In order for us to walk out the purpose and plan that God has for our lives, we must be people of vision. As you will see throughout the rest of this book, having a vision does not necessarily mean that we have all the answers. What it does mean is that God has given us some indication of the future that is ahead of us.

To understand and grasp the importance of vision, it is needful for us to investigate briefly what the Bible has to say about vision. By doing so, we can begin to lay a framework for understanding some of the unwritten reasons that Joseph was able to endure. The other benefit to understanding the principles of vision is we may develop a few critical revelations that will assist us in persevering on our way to destiny.

GOD'S PRINCIPLES

Vision places proper godly restraints on our lives.

Understanding vision requires us to know that what is recorded is what will be remembered.

**The dream we have comes from God
and is intended to be an answer to a question
or a problem in the world around us.**

**Every vision has an aim, target, or goal,
an appointed time for fulfillment, and is always moving
towards its fulfillment whether we realize it or not.**

The first principle of vision is that **vision places proper godly restraints on our lives.** In other words, vision helps us to set appropriate boundaries for what we will do and not do. Proverbs 29:18 says, "Where there is no vision, the people are unrestrained" (NASB). This cannot be overstated. Vision is a critical aspect of our lives as children of God. We must have something of godly significance in front of us that affects our long-term and daily decision-making process. We will see evidence of this in the life of Joseph as we continue to study it. What we will observe from his life and be able to practice in our own lives is the discipline of knowing what to say yes to and what to say no to based on where God is taking us.

The second and third principles of vision can be found in Habakkuk 2:2-3.

> *Then the Lord answered me and said, "Record the vision
> And inscribe it on tablets, that the one who reads it may
> run. For the vision is yet for the appointed time; It hastens
> toward the goal and it will not fail. Though it tarries, wait
> for it; for it will certainly come, it will not delay."*

Understanding vision requires us to know that what is recorded is what will be remembered. Very simply put, it is wise that we have a place to write down the things that we believe God is revealing to us about our future.

One of the major reasons understanding vision is important is because of the way the word vision is translated in other versions of the Bible. This book is not intended to be a theological exposition. With that said, we see the word vision is translated as "revelation"[5] and "answer"[6] in other versions of the Bible. This is important because these two translations help us to understand that **the dream that we have comes from God and is intended to be an answer to a question or a problem in the world around us**. This will be clearly evident in the life of Joseph as we examine it further.

The next principle we can observe from this scripture is that **every vision has an appointed time for fulfillment**. Grasping vision and its relationship to God's timing is crucial for the developing and maintaining of our faith as we continue to pursue all that God has for our lives. God is so detail-oriented and precise in His assignment for us that He works out everything so things will be manifested at their proper time in our lives.

It is important to also note several other elements of vision we can draw from this particular passage. **Vision always has an aim, target, or goal.** The question becomes for us, who is the one who should be setting the target or the goal for the dream God has placed in our hearts. The key to answering this question is asking ourselves if we are willing to develop flexibility. When God gives us a vision, there is nothing wrong with healthy ambition. The key is having the flexibility to remember that God sets the ultimate goal for what fulfillment looks like in our life.

It is also critical to understand that **when God sets a vision or dream in motion, it is always moving towards its fulfillment whether we realize it or not**. It is needful to understand this so we will not value sight over significance. God wants to do something amazing in and through our lives. With this understanding, we cannot allow ourselves to remain discouraged on the way to our destiny. While it is true we will have periods and moments of discouragement on our journey to seeing our dream become our destiny, we cannot allow moments to become a lifetime. If we do, we will miss the many growth opportunities God has engraved within the fabric of the experiences that He permits us to go through.

---

[5] NIV

[6] NLT

In closing this chapter and preparing to re-enter the life of Joseph, I want to challenge you to begin to think about the major things that God has placed on your heart and mind to do. Consider the dreams that are in your heart and realize they seldom come about in the way we may expect or believe they will. Life tends to hand us surprises and things we do not expect. The good news is that though these things may be a surprise to us, they are never a surprise to God. With that, I challenge you to buckle your seatbelt and hold on to your God-given dreams and vision as Joseph did. It may not be easy, but it will certainly be worth it.

Prayer

Father, thank You for every vision and dream that You have placed in my heart. Help me to hold on to what You have shown me even if I do not fully understand it or its significance. Remind me daily that You have placed within me something that will ultimately provide a solution and an answer to the world around me. When I am weak and may not believe, help me to remain faithful to You and to the assignment that You have given me. I trust that You are faithful to bring to completion every intent that You have for my life. In Jesus' name, Amen.

REVIEW GOD'S PRINCIPLES

Here are the important principles God has revealed to us in that chapter.

+ **Vision places proper godly restraints on our lives.**

+ **Understanding vision requires us to know that what is recorded is what will be remembered.**

+ **The dream we have comes from God and is intended to be an answer to a question or a problem in the world around us.**

✦ **Every vision has an aim, target, or goal, an appointed time for fulfillment, and is always moving towards its fulfillment whether we realize it or not**.

Reflect on how these principles encourage you on your personal journey living on the edge of destiny and how to correctly understand and handle the dreams and vision given to you by God.

Chapter 4

DIVINE DETOURS: WHEN IT SEEMS LIKE IT'S ALL OVER, IT REALLY ISN'T

O ne of the most challenging things in our lives is when we hit unexpected adverse circumstances. The reason this can be disheartening is because we often live with an expectation of what we think will occur in our lives, yet we are unaware of the journey that it will take to get there. What we discover in the life of Joseph as well as our own lives is that life can be full of detours.

Merriam Webster's dictionary defines a detour as *a deviation from a direct course or the usual procedure.* As we will observe in the life of Joseph, life seldom provides a direct route to the destiny that God has planned for our lives.

GOD'S PRINCIPLES

Sometimes, we encounter the unexpected in the midst of conducting the routine.

If you have ever felt as though you had great expectations, but something occurred to lead you to believe that all hope was lost, this chapter is for you. If you have ever been in a seemingly hopeless situation and thought that it was the end, this chapter is for you. Hang on in there. It is not over.

In this chapter, we will examine briefly the first detour that Joseph experienced in his life. By doing so, we will discover some difficult truths and principles that will help us to develop the endurance to trust God no matter what. **Sometimes we encounter the unexpected in the midst of conducting the routine.**

As we resume examining Joseph's life, we find him in the midst of completing what appears to have been a normal assignment from his father.

> *Then his brothers went to pasture their father's flock in Shechem. Israel said to Joseph, "Are not your brothers pasturing the flock in Shechem? Come, and I will send you to them." And he said to him, "I will go." Then he said to him, "Go now and see about the welfare of your brothers and the welfare of the flock, and bring word back to me." So he sent him from the valley of Hebron, and he came to Shechem.* (Genesis 37:12-14 NASB).

We may infer that Joseph was at times put in a no-win situation by his father. His brothers were prone to not necessarily doing the things that their father wanted them to do. We can see this in the fact that Joseph frequently reported back to their father poorly in regards to whatever his brothers were doing. With that understanding, we can read the above passage and see that Israel is sending Joseph as he usually did to check on his brothers and to bring back a report of their welfare.

Understand that in this passage, Joseph is headed out to do what was relatively normal and routine for him. However, with that, we begin to see the beginnings of where everything would change for him. The first thing that we can observe is that Joseph's brothers were out of position. In other words, they are not where they are supposed to be.

> *A man found him, and behold, he was wandering in the field; and the man asked him, "What are you looking for?" He said, "I am looking for my brothers; please tell me where they are pasturing the flock." Then the man said,*

"They have moved from here; for I heard them say, 'Let us go to Dothan.'" So Joseph went after his brothers and found them at Dothan. (Genesis 37:15-17 NASB)

Before we go any further, it must be stated that Joseph's brothers not doing whatever it was that they were supposed to be doing was a regular occurrence.

As Joseph approaches his brothers, they see him coming. Take a close look at how they react.

When they saw him from a distance and before he came close to them, they plotted against him to put him to death. They said to one another, "Here comes this dreamer! Now then, come and let us kill him and throw him into one of the pits; and we will say, 'A wild beast devoured him.' Then let us see what will become of his dreams!" (Genesis 37:18-20 NASB).

Joseph's life will be changed forever by what happens next. We can see that his brothers only refer to him as "that dreamer." We often learn the hard way that **people remember our dreams whether they like them or not.** It is probably hard for any of us to imagine our family members hating us so much that they plot to kill us. It should be noted here, however, that earlier we discovered that Joseph's dreams had already caused his brothers to both hate him and be jealous of Him.

Understanding the wording of this plot is interesting. The brothers plan to kill him and they say, "Let's see what becomes of his dreams." This important because when we experience attacks in our life, no matter where they are coming from, we must understand what is actually being attacked. It is also important to understand what our attacker is really after. We will see that the plot thickens even further.

GOD'S PRINCIPLES

People remember our dreams whether they like them or not.

But Reuben heard this and rescued him out of their hands and said, "Let us not take his life." Reuben further said to them, "Shed no blood. Throw him into this pit that is in the wilderness, but do not lay hands on him"—that he might rescue him out of their hands, to restore him to his father. (Genesis 37:21-22 NASB)

It appears that one of Joseph's brothers has a conscience. Reuben didn't want Joseph dead, so he devised a plan to protect him and get him back to his father. What happens next is most interesting.

So it came about, when Joseph reached his brothers, that they stripped Joseph of his tunic, the varicolored tunic that was on him; and they took him and threw him into the pit. Now the pit was empty, without any water in it. (Genesis 37:23-24 NASB)

Whether we realize it or not several things are happening here. First, **just because you are stripped of your possessions, it doesn't mean you have been stripped of your assignment. Just because you lost your stuff doesn't mean you lost your significance.** His brothers stripped him of the coat that his father gave him. Think about this. They decided that before they threw him the pit that they were going to take the physical symbol of his favor. **People may be able to take your things, but they cannot take your favor.**

GOD'S PRINCIPLES

Just because you are stripped of your possessions, it doesn't mean you have been stripped of your assignment or lost your significance.

The next thing we see is the sheer ruthlessness and hatred of Joseph's brothers caused them to throw him a pit with no water in it. Imagine what it must have felt like to be Joseph. He has had dreams regarding his future, yet his present looks nothing like what has been promised. He has seen a glimpse of his future, yet he is in a pit with no hope and no water. This next passage provides us with further insight into the mindset of Joseph's brothers, but does not give us much of a glimpse into Joseph's perception.

Then they sat down to eat a meal. And as they raised their eyes and looked, behold, a caravan of Ishmaelites was coming from Gilead, with their camels bearing aromatic gum and balm and [myrrh, on their way to bring them down to Egypt. Judah said to his brothers, "What profit is it for us to kill our brother and cover up his blood? Come and let us sell him to the Ishmaelites and not lay our hands on him, for he is our brother, our own flesh." And his brothers listened to him. Then some Midianite traders passed by, so they pulled him up and lifted Joseph out of the pit, and sold him to the Ishmaelites for twenty shekels of silver. Thus they brought Joseph into Egypt.

Now Reuben returned to the pit, and behold, Joseph was not in the pit; so he tore his garments. He returned to his brothers and said, "The boy is not there; as for me, where am I to go?" So they took Joseph's tunic, and slaughtered a male goat and dipped the tunic in the blood; and they sent the varicolored tunic and brought it to their father and said, "We found this; please examine it to see whether it is your son's tunic or not." Then he examined it and said, "It is my son's tunic. A wild beast has devoured him; Joseph has surely been torn to pieces!" So Jacob tore his clothes, and put sackcloth on his loins and mourned for his son many days. Then all his sons and all his daughters arose to comfort him, but he refused to be comforted. And he said, "Surely I will go down to Sheol in mourning for my son." So his father wept for him. Meanwhile, the Midianites sold him in Egypt to Potiphar, Pharaoh's officer, the captain of the bodyguard. (Genesis 37:25-36NASB).

GOD'S PRINCIPLES

Sometimes, when we think we are surrendering to our circumstances, we are truly surrendering to God's sovereign plan.

It is never over until God says it over.

One of the biggest proofs of our faith is what we do when we have seemingly no control over our circumstances. Think about how Joseph seemingly has no choice but to surrender to his circumstances. Herein we find a hard truth and a necessary principle. **Sometimes, when we think we are surrendering to our circumstances, we are truly surrendering to God's sovereign plan.** Joseph's brothers are seemingly so heartless that they throw him in a pit and then enjoy a meal. What happens next is eye-opening.

Joseph's brothers next decided that instead of killing him, they should sell him and make a profit off of him. Sometimes, we can read the Bible and not really get the full effect of what is actually happening. Simply put, they thought, *why kill him when we can make some money off of him?* These are his brothers. Imagine people being so hateful and jealous of your God-given dream that they vacillate between killing you and selling you.

The final part of the plot of Joseph's brothers is to take his coat, dip it in blood, and deceive his father into believing that he is dead. This plan seemingly works to perfection and the brothers receive their freedom from Joseph's dreams, or so they thought.

What we can learn from the life of Joseph is that **it is never over until God says it over.** God still had a plan for Joseph's life. Let me remind you that you are not leaving this earth until you accomplish everything that God intends for you to accomplish. Even if it seems hopeless for you right now, God is firmly in control.

We close this chapter with two interesting occurrences. First, the very brothers who plot to kill Joseph but instead sell him are now offering fake concern to cover up what really occurred. They do this by bringing the very coat given to Joseph by his father right back to him with blood on it. The second thing that occurs is that Joseph is sold again to an Egyptian named Potiphar.

Let me make this plain and attempt to share this from what may have been Joseph's perspective. In a short period of time, Joseph goes from living as his father's favorite son to being thrown in a pit by his brothers to be left for dead. It doesn't stop there. He then is drawn out of the pit by the brothers who threw him in there only to be sold for a profit. He is then sold again. Joseph is probably thinking, "God, you gave me a dream. My own brothers don't believe in me. They want me dead. The people they sold me to don't want me." Imagine experiencing this.

Here are some concluding principles that can help us to make the best of the seasons that it seems as if all hope is lost. Things may not work out immediately, but with God, they will always work out eventually.

GOD'S PRINCIPLES

**God doesn't always take us the easiest route,
but He does take us the best route.**

When you cannot see the outcome, trust God anyway.

Prayer

Father, thank You for the opportunity to grow and learn. Help me to surrender to Your plan and Your purpose even when it looks nothing like what I perceived Your promise to be. I know You have a definite plan for my life. I know that with You, I ultimately will see the dream and the vision You have intended for my life fulfilled. Help me to trust when I hit twists and turns. Help me to remain focused on You and faithful to the good that I know to do. When I feel abandoned, please comfort me so I do not abandon Your assignment for my life, in Jesus' name, Amen.

REVIEW GOD'S PRINCIPLES

Here are the important principles God has revealed to us in that chapter.

+ **Just because you are stripped of your possessions doesn't mean you have been stripped of your assignment and doesn't mean you lost your significance.**

+ **People may be able to take your things, but they cannot take your favor.**

+ **Sometimes, when we think we are surrendering to our circumstances, we are truly surrendering to God's sovereign plan.**

+ **It is never over until God says it over.**

+ **God doesn't always take us the easiest route, but He does take us the best route.**

+ **When you cannot see the outcome, trust God anyway.**

Reflect on how these principles encourage you on your personal journey living on the edge of destiny and how to correctly handle the twists and turns you encounter along the way.

Chapter 5

THE POWER OF INTEGRITY

B efore we return to our study of the life of Joseph, we will
spend the next two chapters dealing with two important character traits that must be developed in the life of the person who is
to fulfill the dream and the vision God has for their lives. In this
chapter, we will take a brief look at what the Bible has to say about
integrity. In the next chapter, we will examine the essential quality
of faithfulness. With that foundation, we will revisit Joseph's life
in chapter seven and see how these qualities played a crucial role
in God using him at every stage of his life.

What Is Integrity?

The Merriam-Webster Dictionary defines integrity as the
quality or state of being undivided. It also describes this word as
carrying with it the idea of firm *adherence to a code of especially
moral or artistic values.*[7] What does the Bible convey regarding
integrity? Proverbs 10:9 says, *"He who walks in integrity walks
securely, But he who perverts his ways will be found out"* (NASB).
The biblical idea of integrity as described in this passage carries
the meaning a little further. *Integrity* is biblically defined as *blame-
lessness, innocence, and the state of moral goodness.*

---

[7] Merriam-Webster.com

Understanding both the secular and spiritual definitions of integrity help us to put into perspective the importance of this character trait in the life of the child of God.

GOD'S PRINCIPLES

A life of integrity brings a life of security.

Integrity serves as a moral compass guiding our decisions. When we are not sure what to do, we can always follow the path of integrity.

As we will discover in the life of Joseph, integrity is not a promise that we will never be accused of wrongdoing. Rather it is a guarantee we will ultimately be vindicated by the fulfillment of the plan and purpose God has for our lives. **Thus, it brings a life of security.**

The second principle of integrity is shown in Proverbs 11:3. *"The integrity of the upright will guide them, But the crookedness of the treacherous will destroy them"* (NASB). There are many times in our lives in which the decision we need to make is not immediately clear. Oftentimes, this is easily settled by following the path that demonstrates the most integrity. In other words, **integrity serves as a moral compass providing instruction and direction in situations that are both simple and complex.**

It should be stated that there will be times in which integrity carries a very high price tag. Integrity is not a promise of no problems, but a promise that if we walk honestly, we will outlast every obstacle. Proverbs 28:6 says, *"Better is the poor who walks in his integrity Than he who is crooked though he be rich"* (NASB). Integrity always reminds us not to make permanent choices based on temporary pleasures and circumstances.

GOD'S PRINCIPLES

Integrity has a value that outlasts riches.

Integrity brings with it the promise of generational blessing.

Integrity is important for a lot of reasons, but one of the most significant reasons is because it provides not only a benefit for us but for others. Proverbs 20:7 says, *"A righteous man who walks in his integrity—How blessed are his sons after him"* (NASB). **Integrity brings with it the promise of generational blessing.** This cannot be emphasized nearly enough. When we choose a life of integrity, we are providing a godly example for those coming after us. What a great and lasting blessing it is when we choose to live a life that will provide a pathway for living for our children.

GOD'S PRINCIPLES

**The best time to make a decision is
before we actually have to make it.**

**We may not always be able to start over,
but we can always start where we are.**

As we close this chapter, it must be understood that integrity is simple but seldom easy. Here is a critical principle that we can apply that will assist us in living with integrity on a daily basis. **The best time to make a decision is before we actually have to make it.** It is important to develop a set of godly principles that we will live by. It is important that we are people of strong biblical conviction. It is needful because when difficult situations arise, we will have a preset, default set of values by which we can properly evaluate a situation and know what the godly decision is to make.

As we will see in the life of Joseph, this was a huge part of his success. When he was presented with situations which we will explore in further detail, we always find him acting and choosing the path of integrity. Integrity always has lasting value, but it requires we choose not to live short-sighted lives. Integrity demands we have what pleases God in mind.

It is at this point, I need to give you a word of encouragement. As you read this you might be feeling as though you have stumbled in the area of integrity. Here is the principle to remember: **We may not always be able to start over, but we can always start where we are.** The reality is we cannot live in a yesterday that we cannot change, but we can begin living today to create a better tomorrow for ourselves and our families.

GOD'S PRINCIPLES

To live with integrity, there must be consistency between our words and our actions.

The final principle of integrity relates to the alignment of our words and our actions. Proverbs 19:1 says, *"Better is a poor man who walks in his integrity than he who is perverse in speech and is a fool"* (NASB). **To live with integrity, there must be consistency between our words and our actions.** One of the greatest challenges to our Christian walk from those who look on from the outside is when we live in a way that is inconsistent with what we claim to believe. This means we must be people who weigh heavily what we do, what we preach, and what we practice.

The starting place for developing a life of integrity is surrender. As we are willing to commit to living our life in the light of God's ways rather than our own preferences, He will bring us to the place we need to be and help us to remain faithful to the godly value that will bring Him glory.

You will see in the life of Joseph that integrity is often very difficult. We cannot allow the challenges of integrity to cause us to forfeit the greater good and ultimate plan of God for our lives just because the wrong choice is easier. Decide today that the path of integrity, no matter how difficult, is ultimately the best choice.

Prayer

Father, I ask You to forgive me of every area in which I may lack integrity. Help me to develop godly values and principles by which I can live a life that is most pleasing to You. Give me an accurate moral compass. I know that as I walk with integrity, I will live in ultimate vindication and security. Integrity begins with surrender, therefore, I surrender my life, actions, thoughts, and words completely to You and trust You to help me daily to walk out what You have worked into my life. Lord, give me complete alignment between my words and my actions. Help me to live in a way that I am not accused of being inconsistent in my lifestyle which I proclaim with my words.

REVIEW GOD'S PRINCIPLES

Here are the important principles God has revealed to us in that chapter.

✦ **A life of integrity brings a life of security.**

✦ **Integrity serves as a moral compass guiding our decisions. When we are not sure what to do, we can always follow the path of integrity.**

✦ **Integrity has a value that outlasts riches.**

✦ **Integrity brings with it the promise of generational blessing.**

✦ **The best time to make a decision is before we actually have to make it.**

✦ **We may not always be able to start over, but we can always start where we are.**

✦ **To live with integrity, there must be consistency between our words and our actions.**

Reflect on how these principles encourage you on your personal journey living on the edge of destiny and how to live your life with godly integrity.

Chapter 6
CHOOSING FAITHFULNESS

I n this chapter, we will give a brief overview of another essential quality that we will discover in the life of Joseph. Faithfulness is non-negotiable in fulfilling the dream and vision God has for our lives. This is not intended to be an exhaustive study of faithfulness. I want to just highlight a few key principles that the Word of God provides regarding this most needful character trait.

Paul writes in 1 Corinthians 4:2, "*Now it is required that those who have been given a trust must prove faithful*" (NIV). **Whenever we are given an assignment or responsibility, it is an opportunity to practice and model faithfulness.** We must clearly understand faithfulness is not a suggestion when it comes to the fulfillment of the purpose, dream, and vision that God has for our lives. It is an essential requirement. This is important to understand since we can sometimes observe from our culture, a lack of stability. In many instances, whenever something becomes unpleasant or one loses interest, the task is abandoned and one becomes unfaithful.

GOD'S PRINCIPLES

Whenever we are given an assignment or responsibility, it is an opportunity to practice and model faithfulness.

Integrity cannot be separated from faithfulness. In most cases, they operate as two sides of the same coin.

Faithfulness in its simplest terms refers to the character trait of being both trustworthy and reliable. Our level of faithfulness may be the single most significant thing that people remember about us. So, what will you be known for? What will your reputation be? It has been said that our character is more important than our reputation. I would challenge this assumption slightly. I submit to you that character is the foundation of our reputation. When we choose to be people of integrity, faithfulness naturally follows. **Integrity cannot be separated from faithfulness. In most cases, they operate as two sides of the same coin.** In short, who we are and what we value undergirds what we do and how we do it daily.

GOD'S PRINCIPLES

We must always choose to be faithful and trustworthy in whatever we have to do, regardless of how we perceive its importance.

Sometimes, the greatest tests we experience in our lives are found in seemingly small matters.

The next principle of faithfulness is **we must always choose to be faithful and trustworthy in whatever we have to do, regardless of how we perceive its importance.** Jesus expressed in Matthew 25:21, *"His master replied, 'Well done, good and faithful servant! You have been faithful with a few things; I will put you in charge of many things. Come and share your master's happiness!'"* (NIV). **Sometimes, the greatest tests we will experience in our lives are found in seemingly small matters.**

One of the harshest realities we must face is that we do not always know when we are being tested and we do not always know what is being tested. This is a major point that cannot be ignored. This is exactly why we must be faithful in everything we do.

What we learn from the above passage is that promotion is often a result of how we handle where we are. Moving forward in our lives and moving closer to the vision and the dream God has for us is often the fruit of faithfully dealing with our current circumstances. One thing we will observe when we continue looking at the life of Joseph is that he was uncompromisingly faithful in everything that he did. The other thing we tend to over-look look is that Joseph proved faithful in his assignments even without promises of promotion or freedom. What this indicates to us is that Joseph's choice to live faithfully and honestly regardless of his circumstances was much more about his relationship with God than it was about his relationship with his future.

A point of clarity must be made here. We are not suggesting that one should not be concerned with their future. We are also not suggesting that one should not try to advance in various aspects of their life. What we are saying is that our ultimate reason for living and walking in both integrity and faithfulness is that we honor and glorify God in all that we do. Paul further illustrates the importance of this concept in Colossians 3:23-24.

> **Whatever you do, work at it with all your heart, as working for the Lord,** *not for human masters, since you know that you will receive an inheritance from the Lord as a reward. It is the Lord Christ you are serving.* (NIV emphasis added)

Think about what Paul is saying here and how it further supports what has been described in this chapter thus far. In essence, Paul tells us it is not only important what we do, but it is equally important how we do it. It is of further profound importance to have a clear awareness of whom we are doing it for.

As we will see in Joseph's life and what we can apply to our own lives, we must always do our best work and give it our all. The ultimate reason for choosing to always put forth our best effort is the understanding that what we do is service to the Lord. The mistake we can make in our own lives is to believe that work inside of the church and Christian community is the only thing that can be considered service to God. The spiritual reality is that everything we do should be done in the light of our relationship with the Lord. When we consider that our walk with the Lord should inform and motivate all that we do, it will change our perspective on both our circumstances and our actions.

GOD'S PRINCIPLES

**When we serve God faithfully, we will discover
every circumstance ultimately becomes an opportunity.**

We must ask ourselves if that is how we have lived our lives up to this point. If we have not been faithful, we have an opportunity to begin now. As children of God, we do not only want our work to speak for us, but ultimately, we want it to speak for God. What an amazing testimony we will have when we can say I have been faithful, trustworthy, and have given our all. The beauty of this is that even when things do not go as planned or turn out as we might have liked them to, we can know on the inside that we have given our very best effort to do things in a way that would honor God.

In the next chapter, we will resume our journey through the life of Joseph. As we look at his life in the light of the importance of faithfulness and integrity, you will be inspired by how he lived his life to realize that you can outlast every obstacle and you can turn every occurrence into an opportunity for God to be glorified. I want to challenge you to always choose faithfulness. Like every quality that we are able to highlight from the life of Joseph, we may not always see and feel the immediate results, but we will always experience the eventual results.

Prayer

Father, I thank You for revealing to me the importance and necessity of faithfulness. Help me to look at every activity that I undertake each day as an opportunity to be faithful and trustworthy. Give me a continued awareness that what I do in this life I do for You. Help me to realize that though I may not have control of my immediate circumstances, I am never a slave to those circumstances. Help me to fulfill my commitment to You above all else. I ask that as I live for You, people will see my works and look at them as a reflection of Your grace, Your empowerment, and Your glory. In Jesus' name, Amen.

REVIEW GOD'S PRINCIPLES

Here are the important principles God has revealed to us in that chapter.

✦ **Whenever we are given an assignment or responsibility, it is an opportunity to practice and model faithfulness.**

✦ **Integrity cannot be separated from faithfulness. In most cases, they operate as two sides of the same coin.**

✦ **We must always choose to be faithful and trustworthy in whatever we have to do regardless of how we perceive its importance.**

✦ **Sometimes, the greatest tests we will experience in our lives are found in seemingly small matters.**

✦ **When we serve God faithfully, we will discover every circumstance ultimately becomes an opportunity.**

Reflect on how these principles encourage you on your personal journey living on the edge of destiny and how to do everything faithfully as unto the Lord.

Chapter 7

IT'S JUST NOT FAIR
BUT HE IS RIGHT THERE

W hat do you do when life just doesn't seem fair? How do you remain confident in God when things don't go as expected? One of the major themes of Joseph's life is that we are hard-pressed to find anything going routinely or as planned or expected. In the previous two chapters, we discussed the important character traits we will see played out going forward in the exploration of Joseph's life—integrity and faithfulness.

What becomes increasingly clear is that while he could not control the things that happened to him, he chose to control his responses to them. If we examine our own lives, more often than not we will learn the same truth. It is impossible for us to personally predict all we may face in our lives, but when we make a decision to follow the path of integrity and faithfulness, God will take care of us.

As we begin this chapter, we pick up Joseph's life after he has been sold to an Egyptian named Potiphar. It is through this experience that Joseph will demonstrate the necessary qualities of a person who will see the mandate, dream, vision, and assignment of God in his life fulfilled. As we look at this, we can glean several principles that will help us in our own journey toward destiny and purpose. The other notable thing we will learn in this chapter is we can do what is right and still end up being treated seemingly unfairly. However, no matter what we experience, we can be fully confident that God is firmly in control.

Genesis 39:1-2 gives us some immediate insight into one of the key elements that define Joseph's life. While we can extract certain qualities and characteristics of Joseph's life, what we will see in these verses lays the ultimate foundation for Joseph's success.

Now Joseph had been taken down to Egypt; and Potiphar, an Egyptian officer of Pharaoh, the captain of the bodyguard, bought him from the Ishmaelites, who had taken him down there. **The Lord was with Joseph, so he became a successful man.** *And he was in the house of his master, the Egyptian.* (NASB emphasis added)

GOD'S PRINCIPLES

**It does not matter what our circumstances are.
What matters is who is with us
in the midst of those circumstances.**

The ultimate source of our success is the presence of God.

**Success resides in the hands of God.
No matter what we go through,
if we are faithful and walk with integrity, He will protect us.**

What we are told about Joseph in this passage is that the Lord was with him and that is why he was successful. We cannot overlook the significance of what is said here. Because of the presence of God in Joseph's life, he was not a slave to his circumstances. What can we learn from this is that no matter how many qualities we possess and no matter how much good we do, **the ultimate source of our success is the presence of God**. Our character and integrity can certainly position us, but we can never lose sight of the fact that success comes from God.

He holds success in store for the upright, he is a shield to those whose walk is blameless, for he guards the course of the just and protects the way of his faithful ones." (Proverbs 2:7-8 NIV)

Here is the principle that we will begin to see unfold next in the life of Joseph. **Success resides in the hands of God. No matter what we go through, if we are faithful and walk with integrity, He will protect us.** One cannot take an honest look at the life of Joseph without seeing the truth that God is faithful and He is in charge.

GOD'S PRINCIPLES

The presence of God produces a result that is visible to others.

The presence of God working in our lives will give us all the necessary favor that we need with others.

Now his master saw that the Lord was with him and how the Lord caused all that he did to prosper in his hand. So Joseph found favor in his sight and became his personal servant; and he made him overseer over his house, and all that he owned he put in his charge. (Genesis 39:3-4 NASB emphasis added)

It is in these verses that we begin to see the fruit and effect of the presence of God on the life of Joseph. What we just read is powerful and in it, we see several principles that we can draw from the life of Joseph. First, **the presence of God produced a result that was visible to others.** The Bible tells us that Potiphar noticed the presence of God in Joseph's life. It further tells us that Potiphar noticed that whatever Joseph did was prosperous.

The next principle we can observe from these verses is that **the presence of God working in our lives will give us all the necessary favor that we need with others.** We can see from the

43

above passage that because God was present with Joseph, he was the recipient of man's favor and he was promoted. Whenever we find ourselves in adverse circumstances or in things we cannot control, we can rely on the presence of God to lead us, guide us, and direct us. We can also be certain that it is God's hand upon our lives and our God-directed actions that will give us success and produce the favor necessary to progress further toward our dreams and destiny.

The fruit of the presence of God in the life of Joseph is further highlighted in Genesis 39:5-6.

> *It came about that from the time he made him overseer in his house and over all that he owned, **the Lord blessed** the Egyptian's house on account of Joseph; thus **the Lord's blessing** was upon all that he owned, in the house and in the field. So he left everything he owned in Joseph's charge; and with him there he did not concern himself with anything except the food which he ate.* (Genesis 39:5-6 NASB emphasis added)

What we are seeing is absolutely astounding. Potiphar's house experiences blessing in every single area simply because he made a decision to recognize the presence of God in Joseph's life and position him properly. The house was blessed beyond measure because Joseph was in it.

It is at this point, we come back to the truth that things do not always go as we think they will. From every conceivable angle, all is going well for Joseph and all is going well for Potiphar. Joseph has made the absolute best of a bad situation. He has been sold twice and now he has found a place of stability and seeming significance in the house of Potiphar. It is here where we find that Joseph's life is about to take another huge detour.

> *Now Joseph was handsome in form and appearance. It came about after these events that his master's wife looked with desire at Joseph, and she said, "Lie with me." **But he refused** and said to his master's wife, "Behold, with me*

here, my master does not concern himself with anything in the house, and he has put all that he owns in my charge. There is no one greater in this house than I, and he has withheld nothing from me except you because you are his wife. How then could I do this great evil and sin against God? (Genesis 39:6b-9 NASB emphasis added)

Apparently, Joseph did not just do his job well, he was also a good-looking fellow. The above passage demonstrates to us that Joseph was a man of integrity. Potiphar's wife began to desire Joseph and made advances toward him. Joseph's response to this says a lot about the integrity that he developed in his life up to this point.

Joseph expresses to Potiphar's wife that he could not give in to her temptations because to do so would be a sin and a violation against God. In other words, Joseph realized that everything that he did in his life was a reflection of his relationship and connection to God.

GOD'S PRINCIPLES

A life of integrity honors God. Every decision we make in our life is a reflection of the strength and depth of our relationship with Him.

Integrity is not a promise that things will always go smoothly, always go fairly, and always go easy.

We must understand that with every temptation, God has an escape route, but it is up to us to take it.

One can walk in complete integrity and still be falsely accused of doing wrong.

As she spoke to Joseph day after day, he did not listen to her to lie beside her or be with her. Now it happened one day that he went into the house to do his work, and none of the men of the household was there inside. She caught him by his garment, saying, "Lie with me!" And he left his garment in her hand and fled, and went outside. (Genesis 39:10-12 NASB)

We can see from these verses that **we will have to resist seen frequently and often.** Potiphar's wife continued to pursue Joseph in the same fashion daily. Joseph is so full of integrity, he runs from the situation in order to avoid sinning against God and Potiphar.

What we learn from the life of Joseph is that there will be times we have to take extreme measures to remove ourselves from situations that could cause us to sin and to stumble. Paul said in 1 Corinthians 10:13, *"No temptation has overtaken you but such as is common to man; and God is faithful, who will not allow you to be tempted beyond what you are able, but with the temptation will provide the way of escape also, so that you will be able to endure it"* (NIV).

We must understand that with every temptation, God has an escape route, but it is up to us to take it. Joseph was wise in running away from a situation that may have caused him to sin, but his integrity was no promise that he would not endure suffering for making the right decision. What happens next is unthinkable.

She called to the men of her household and said to them, "See, he has brought in a Hebrew to us to make sport of us; he came in to me to lie with me, and I screamed. When he heard that I raised my voice and screamed, he left his garment beside me and fled and went outside." So she left his garment beside her until his master came home. Then she spoke to him [with these words], "The Hebrew slave, whom you brought to us, came in to me to make sport of me; and as I raised my voice and screamed, he left his garment beside me and fled outside." (Genesis 39:14-18 NASB)

One can walk in complete integrity and still be falsely accused of doing wrong. We have no idea what the true motivation was behind Potiphar's wife creating a situation and scenario by which she could falsely accuse Joseph. Perhaps, she was humiliated that Joseph rejected her advances. This seems to be the most likely scenario. The scheme laid out by Potiphar's wife did not end with sharing this false story with the other men associated with the household.

> *Now when his master heard the words of his wife, which she spoke to him, saying, "This is what your slave did to me," his anger burned. So Joseph's master took him and put him into the jail, the place where the king's prisoners were confined; and he was there in the jail.* (Genesis 39:19-20 NASB)

Potiphar's wife relays the same story to her husband. We are told from the scripture that Potiphar was extremely angry. What is unclear from the text is what the true source of anger was a belief that Joseph actually did what he was accused of or whether it was the fact that the accusation was even made.

It seems unlikely that Potiphar would easily believe that someone he trusted with everything in his house but his food would be capable of what he was being accused of. We only see that the result of these accusations lands Joseph in prison for something that he did not do.

The ultimate question we must answer for ourselves is what do we do when we are hit with things that are totally unfair? What happens when we end up like Joseph? What do we do when we have done all that we know how to do to live with integrity and that integrity does not seem to pay us back?

As we close this chapter, it is important to remember a few things. First, **when life does not seem fair or make sense, our response and posture must be complete trust.** What we can see with each detour that occurred in Joseph's life, were twists he could not possibly have planned for. It would be foolish for us to believe that the things he experienced did not have an effect on him.

Perhaps, you are reading this and you can think of a time in which you were wrongly accused of doing something you know you did not door a time when your motives were questioned. These types of events occurring in our lives tend to sting like few other things can. It is at these times, it is easy to become offended and eventually bitter. We cannot be totally sure from the scriptures that this did not occur in Joseph's life. We are not given many details about his response. We are only told that he was placed in prison.

As we consider Joseph's life up to this point, what we can continue to see is that no matter what, God is firmly in control. **Our future is not in the hands of our present circumstances.** We don't know whether Joseph hung onto his dream. We are not given the details of the level of discouragement he may have experienced. What we can observe is that he is trying to do his best and he is suffering for doing what is right.

GOD'S PRINCIPLES

**When life does not seem fair or make sense,
our response and posture must be complete trust in God.**

**Our future is not in the hands of our present circumstances.
God's vision and dream for your life
do not bow to anyone but Him.**

**When we cannot see the way,
we can be assured that God has made a way.
We don't have to know how, we only need to know God.**

I want to encourage you that God is not finished with you. When it appears as if all hope is lost, God still has a plan and God still has a purpose. **God's vision and dream for your life do not bow to anyone but Him.** From our human standpoint, the path to what God has shown us may seem completely impossible. When we feel that way, we must remember that God specializes in the seemingly impossible. **When we cannot see the way, we can be** assured that God has made a way. We don't have to know how, we only need to know God.

Prayer

Father, thank You for allowing me to be alive today. Help me to gain freedom from any offense and bitterness in my mind and heart caused by false accusations, being misunderstood, or being misperceived. Help me to remain full of hope, full of faith, full of trust, and full of integrity as I continue to pursue Your dream and vision for my life. I know You are completely faithful to Your word. I know that since You are faithful, every vision, every promise, and every dream You have authored will be fulfilled in Your perfect timing, In Jesus' name, Amen.

REVIEW GOD'S PRINCIPLES

Here are the important principles God has revealed to us in that chapter.

+ **It does not matter what our circumstances are. What matters is who is with us in the midst of those circumstances.**

+ **The ultimate source of our success is the presence of God.**

+ **Success resides in the hands of God. No matter what we go through, if we are faithful and walk with integrity, He will protect us.**

+ **The presence of God produces a result visible to others and will give us all the necessary favor we need with others.**

+ **Integrity is not a promise that things will always go smoothly, always goes fairly, and always go easy.**

✦ We must understand that with every temptation, God has an escape route, but it is up to us to take it.

✦ One can walk in complete integrity and still be falsely accused of doing wrong.

✦ When life does not seem fair or make sense, our response and posture must be complete trust.

✦ Our future is not in the hands of our present circumstances.

✦ God's vision and dream for your life do not bow to anyone but Him.

✦ When we cannot see the way, we can be assured that God has made a way. We don't have to know how, we only need to know God.

Reflect on how these principles encourage you on your personal journey living on the edge of destiny and how to correctly handle things when life does not seem fair.

Chapter 8

THE PREVAILING POWER OF HUMILITY

We have spent much time thus far looking at important principles from the life of Joseph that will help us in our journey toward the dream and vision that God has for our lives. Within this chapter and the next, we will look at two more specific qualities that Joseph had to develop in order to fulfill the mandate and assignment God had for his life. When we rejoin Joseph in Chapter 10, we will see how the qualities of humility and dependence on God played a critical role in his life.

The purpose of this chapter is to briefly examine humility and understand the crucial role the Bible says that it plays in the life of the child of God. James 4:10 says, *"Humble yourselves before the Lord, and he will lift you up in honor"* (NLT). This statement is simple to grasp, but not necessarily to practice. James shares with us the responsibility we have and the result God promises us.

GOD'S PRINCIPLES

**As we practice humility,
we have a promise that God will promote us.**

In considering the promoting nature and power of God, it is important to note that the principle of humility leading to godly exaltation is universally applicable. Matthew 23:12 expresses,

"Whoever exalts himself shall be humbled; and whoever humbles himself shall be exalted" (NLT).

GOD'S PRINCIPLES

Pride will always seek to promote and exalt self. Humility is willing to surrender to the purpose, plan, and timing of God.

There is no way around the truth that absolute trust and dependency upon God is a crucial trait and quality needed to walk out the dream that God has planned for our lives. We see this point illustrated further in 1 Peter 5:6 which says, *"So humble yourselves under the mighty power of God, and at the right time he will lift you up in honor"* (NLT).

We can see the only proper response to the awareness and knowledge of the presence and power of God is a posture of humility. We have already noted that when we practice humility God will exalt and promote us. Peter, however, adds an interesting caveat to our understanding. God always promotes us in His perfect timing. Trusting God completely often means surrendering our preferred timing to His.

The practice of humility is extremely countercultural. In our world, humility is often proclaimed but rarely practiced. Many tend to shoulder the responsibility and pressure of being noticed for their perceived achievements and accomplishments. We directly or indirectly are encouraged to herald our own greatness. In many world ventures, this appears to be the right path. For the believer, however, the path to greatness is much different.

The next thing that we can discover about humility is that it is possible and preferable for one to be intentional about practicing it. Colossians 3:12 says, *"Since God chose you to be the holy people he loves, you must clothe yourselves with tenderhearted mercy, kindness, humility, gentleness, and patience"* (NLT). This passage provides great insight into the way we should see humility. The idea conveyed is that it is something that we wear. With the intentionality that we put on physical clothing, we must do so even more with our spiritual clothing.

GOD'S PRINCIPLES

It is always better to seek God's way of doing things then it is to simply seek things.

As we continue to consider the idea of humility, a unique thing can be noticed. **It is always better to seek God's way of doing things than it is to simply seek things.** Proverbs 22:4 says, *"True humility and fear of the Lord lead to riches, honor, and long life"* (NLT). The reality that we all must eventually face in our lives is that every path leads somewhere. With that understanding, we want to make sure that the path we choose to take in life is leading us to the places that God wants us to go. The scripture conveys that the path of humility has a reward that comes with it. It promises three things: riches, honor, and life. Think about this for a minute. Many spend their entire life looking to accomplish and get these things on their own without any real or true understanding of what they actually are or how they should fit into our life. God doesn't have an issue with us having things, but humility teaches us that things, tangible or intangible, should never have us.

GOD'S PRINCIPLES

The end result of pride unchecked is disgrace.

**Humility allows us to be teachable
and seek and practice wisdom.
Reverence and respect for the Lord
will lead us to practice wisdom.**

Both pride and humility are conditions of the heart.

We have spoken about the positive aspects of humility. I would like to spend the remainder of this chapter discussing the dangers of not walking with an attitude of humility. A failure to practice humility almost always leads to disastrous consequences. Proverbs 11:2 states, *"Pride leads to disgrace, but with humility comes wisdom"* (NLT). One of the great things about Scripture is that it often makes principles plain and simple for us to see. It is up to us to take what we learn and put it in to practice. We are told here that **the end result of pride unchecked is disgrace.** Who wants disgrace and shame to be their legacy? Making sure this does not happen is hidden in this passage. On the surface, one might think it is just humility. The truth is that **humility allows us to be teachable and seek and practice wisdom.** We will see this later in the life of Joseph. One of the keys to his promotion and success was the combination of wisdom and humility that he practiced regularly in every situation.

As we already saw earlier, the combination of wisdom and humility will lead us to a place of honor in God's eyes and a place of favor with others. Proverbs 15:33 says, *"Fear of the Lord teaches wisdom; humility precedes honor"* (NLT). **Reverence and respect for the Lord will ultimately lead us to practice wisdom.** Humility helps us to understand our need for wisdom and positions us to experience the honor that can only ultimately be bestowed upon us by God.

To further illustrate the dangers of choosing pride over humility, we turn to Proverbs 18:12, *"Before destruction the heart of man is haughty but humility goes before honor"* (NLT). **Both pride and humility are conditions of the heart.** This is very crucial for us to realize. We often focus on behaviors and actions instead of taking an honest look at the reason behind those behaviors and the actions we are taking. This ends up leading to a false humility that intentionally or unintentionally seeks to cover up the true condition of our hearts. To put it plainly, **it all starts with the heart.** The direction of our lives will follow strongly after the direction of our hearts.

In closing this chapter, it is important to note that humility teaches us the lasting and eternal truth that we are not in control, God is in control. As such, we must remain humble and teachable so that we can receive the wisdom and understanding to do everything that God wants us to do in the way that He wants us to do it.

Prayer

Father, please reveal to me any areas of pride that have gone unchecked in my life. Help me to develop and maintain a teach-able heart and spirit so that I may walk in perfect humility and practice the wisdom that You impart into my life. Thank You for using the quality of humility to move me closer to the purpose and dream that You have for my life. In Jesus' name, Amen.

REVIEW GOD'S PRINCIPLES

Here are the important principles God has revealed to us in that chapter.

✦ **As we practice humility, we have a promise that God will promote us.**

✦ **Pride will always seek to promote and exalt self. Humility is willing to surrender to the purpose, plan, and timing of God.**

✦ **It is always better to seek God's way of doing things than it is to simply seek things.**

✦ **The end result of pride unchecked is disgrace.**

✦ **Humility allows us to be teachable and to seek and practice wisdom.**

✦ **Reverence and respect for the Lord will ultimately lead us to practice wisdom.**

✦ **Both pride and humility are conditions of the heart.**

Reflect on how these principles encourage you on your personal journey living on the edge of destiny and how to humbly seek God's promotions and His timing.

Chapter 9

YOU CAN COUNT ON GOD

B efore returning to the life of Joseph, we are going to explore one of the character traits that becomes evident in his life. In this chapter, we will deal with depending on God. This phrase can almost become a cliché. With that said, we tend to depend on resources and other people more than we depend on God. What becomes evident in the life of Joseph is that God allows us to come into situations in which the only person that we can look to for the fulfillment of our purpose in Him.

A major aspect of depending on God is understanding that He is firmly in control of the affairs of our lives. Proverbs 16:9 expresses, "We can make our plans, but the Lord determines our steps" (NLT). It is easy to misunderstand this verse. One might read this and think we should not be diligent in planning and preparation for the things God has given us to do. This could not be further from the truth. The reality is that we must be diligent and demonstrate forethought, but we must also be willing to develop flexibility.

GOD'S PRINCIPLES

**Flexibility places us in the proper posture
by which we can surrender to and trust in God.**

In short, it helps us to do our best while trusting and believing that in all things, God's way is best. This point is further emphasized in Proverbs 19:21, "Many plans are in a man's heart, but the counsel of the Lord will stand" (NASB). It is actually reassuring us to know that as we place our hope and trust in God, He is true to His Word and true to His purpose. Even though we may have many thoughts, feelings, and ideas about what we believe will happen in our lives, it is ultimately God's plan and purpose that will come to pass.

When considering what it means to depend on God, one of the first things we can observe from the Scriptures is that God's ways are always better than ours. With trust in God comes the promise of direction. Proverbs 3:5-6 says, "Trust in the Lord with all your heart; do not depend on your own understanding. Seek his will in all you do, and he will show you which path to take" (NLT).

GOD'S PRINCIPLES

**Our own understanding will never be
more reliable than trust in God.
When we trust God, He will lead us
in the path that we should go.**

Perhaps at this point, you are thinking about many times in your life in which the vision and dream you had from God seemed clear. You may have been starting to chart your preferred course to this dream. Maybe you even wrote down plans, goals, timelines, and milestones. All of these things would help to achieve an optimal conclusion in your undertakings and efforts.

As stated earlier, it is crucial for us to be connected to both God's will and God's way. More often than not, we don't have an issue with our perceived and desired result but with the path that God may take us to get there.

As we will see in the next chapter, Joseph was no different than us. He had a vision of his future, but he had no idea what measures God would take and what circumstances He would allow to occur in his life in order to see that vision come to pass. Joseph would learn, as we must learn, that **when we can't see it, we must still trust.** When things seem uncertain and unstable in our lives, we must continue to completely rely upon God to help us stay strong and develop endurance on our journey to the dream.

As we continue to explore depending on God, I want to encourage you not to allow your faith and hope to rest on any-body or anything but God. Have you ever relied on a person to do something for you? Perhaps you thought that because someone was your friend, they would come through for you in your time of need. Maybe you have a close friend whom you have helped in the past and all of a sudden, they are placed in a position where they can help you or show you favor. Maybe they promised to do it and they even should have done it.

Everyone can likely identify with being in this situation only to discover that the one that they thought was going to make it happen for them didn't come through. We can all remember having this type of disappointing feeling. The good news is that no matter how hurt or discouraged we may have become by be letting down by man, we can still depend on God.

GOD'S PRINCIPLES

Placing trust in man can only provide temporary success and satisfaction at best.

There is always a blessing upon trusting and dependence on God.

We have already established the importance of depending on God. God speaking through the prophet Jeremiah further expresses the importance of this principle.

Thus says the Lord, "Cursed is the man who trusts in mankind. And makes flesh his strength, And whose heart turns away from the Lord. For he will be like a bush in the desert and will not see when prosperity comes, but will live in stony wastes in the wilderness, a land of salt without inhabitant." (Jeremiah 17:5-6 NASB)

Here we discover the absolute necessity of not placing our faith in any human being. The prophet instructs us to understand that placing our faith in man will ultimately lead us to turn away from God. When we place any level of faith intended for God in man, we will ultimately be disappointed.

The good news is there is a lasting blessing and an ultimate reward for trusting God. Jeremiah contrasts the danger of trusting man with the value of trusting in God.

Blessed is the man who trusts in the Lord And whose trust is the Lord. For he will be like a tree planted by the water, that extends its roots by a stream and will not fear when the heat comes; but its leaves will be green, and it will not be anxious in a year of drought nor cease to yield fruit. (Jeremiah 17:7-8 NASB)

There is always a blessing upon trusting and dependence on God. What we can observe from this scripture is that God promises fruitfulness, stability, and prosperity to those who place their faith in Him.

Can you imagine living a life in which your stability and success are based solely upon your dependence and reliance upon God to do what He promised to do? This can be difficult at times, but it is so worth it. Give your heart and mind completely to the plan and the purpose of God.

In giving thought to the previously stated, it should inspire us to continue looking to the Lord to supply everything we need in every area of our life to bring about His intended and desired result. When we surrender to Him and depend on Him this way, we will experience and enjoy true and lasting fruitfulness. As we will see in the next chapter, Joseph learns this painful lesson. We typically learn the lesson of dependence through temporary disappointment.

GOD'S PRINCIPLES

**We can always learn from disappointment,
but we should never live there.**

Prayer

Father, thank You for reminding me of Your goodness and faithfulness. Thank You for giving me an awareness of the importance of placing my faith, hope, and trust in only You. Forgive me for the times and the moments in which I have been tempted to trust things and people more than I trust You. You have a vision, dream, and mission for my life. I am renewing my complete reliability in You to bring that vision and dream to pass.

REVIEW GOD'S PRINCIPLES

Here are the important principles God has revealed to us in that chapter.

✦ **Flexibility places us in the proper posture by which we can surrender to and trust in God.**

✦ **Our own understanding will never be more reliable than trust in God. When we trust God, He will lead us in the path that we should go.**

✦ **Placing trust in man can only provide temporary success and satisfaction at best.**

✦ **There is always a blessing upon trusting and dependence on God.**

✦ **We can always learn from disappointment, but we should never live there.**

Reflect on how these principles encourage you to depend on God and not on man on your personal journey living on the edge of destiny.

Chapter 10

FORGOTTEN BUT NOT FINISHED

W hen we last left Joseph, we found him falsely accused and thrown in prison. It is here that Joseph will begin the fast track to the true purpose God had for his life. While all of the previous stages we have looked at played a key role in getting him to this point, it is in the prison where Joseph's life will take a turn that will set him on a course to his divine destiny.

> *So Joseph's master took him and put him into the jail, the place where the king's prisoners were confined; and he was there in the jail.* ***But the Lord was with Joseph and extended kindness to him, and gave him favor in the sight of the chief jailer.*** *The chief jailer committed to Joseph's charge all the prisoners who were in the jail; so that whatever was done there, he was responsible for it. The chief jailer did not supervise anything under Joseph's charge* ***because the Lord was with him; and whatever he did, the Lord made to prosper.*** (Genesis 39:20-23 NASB).

What we immediately notice is that Joseph leaves a unique impression much different from those around him. The text provides us with insight as to what makes Joseph different from others.

We are told, "the Lord was with Joseph." Make no mistake about it. **The most important factor in accomplishing anything**

for God is His presence. We cannot overlook the fact Joseph had God's presence working in His life even while in a prison. The natural fruit of God's presence and kindness over the life of Joseph was he would again find himself promoted. **God's presence always produces God's favor and God's favor leads to God's promotion.** Take a minute to think about what is actually happening here. God's favor is so strong in the life of Joseph, he becomes a prisoner in charge of other prisoners and is given oversight of everything that happens in the jail.

The next thing you will notice is the same thing we observed while Joseph was serving in Potiphar's house. The passage tells us, *"and whatever he did, the Lord made to prosper."* In short, everything that Joseph undertook was successful. So often, we put our faith and trust in our ability and the ability of others, but ultimately, we need the presence of God to experience success. This is not an excuse to fail to develop needed skills to handle the responsibilities we are given. We just have to do so with the understanding that it is God who makes things prosper.

GOD'S PRINCIPLES

**Your circumstances can never
truly imprison your purpose.
Focus on your purpose and allow
God to deal with your position.**

Then it came about after these things, the cupbearer and the baker for the king of Egypt offended their lord, the king of Egypt. Pharaoh was furious with his two officials, the chief cupbearer and the chief baker. So he put them in confinement in the house of the captain of the bodyguard, in the jail, the same place where Joseph was imprisoned. The captain of the bodyguard put Joseph in charge of them, and he took care of them; and they were in confinement for some time. Then the cupbearer and the baker for the king of Egypt, who were confined in jail, both had a dream the

same night, each man with his own dream and each dream
with its own interpretation. (Genesis 40:1-5)

The king gets ticked off with his baker and his cupbearer and
tosses them in prison. We are not told why. We just know they did
enough to offend him to the point of earning themselves a prison
sentence. This portion of the story actually reveals somethings
about Joseph. We are told that Joseph took care of these two new
prisoners. We can infer from the text that Joseph did not use his
position of authority to throw his power around, but to take the
best care possible of the people under his authority.

GOD'S PRINCIPLES

Use your position and authority in this world to help people.

What happens next is the second phase of something Joseph
has experienced in his life earlier. Both the cupbearer and the
baker have a dream. We are told from the text that each dream
had its own interpretation.

When Joseph came to them in the morning and observed
them, behold, they were dejected. He asked Pharaoh's
officials who were with him in confinement in his master's
house, "Why are your faces so sad today?" Then they
said to him, "We have had a dream and there is no one
to interpret it." Then Joseph said to them, "Do not
interpretations belong to God? Tell it to me, please."
(Genesis 40:6-8 NASB)

Joseph finds these two servants of the king displaying a
demeanor that indicates they are not in the best mental state. The
text calls their appearances "dejected." The word carries with it
the idea of being "thrown down, upset, troubled, and distraught."
This speaks to the value people placed upon dreams at the time.
It is important to note they were not upset with having the dream.
They were troubled because they did not have an interpretation.

Take a close look at Joseph's response. He says, "*Do not inter-pretations belong to God. Tell it to me, please.*" It is interesting to observe that Joseph did not have to show any concern for these prisoners. At this point, he had nothing personally to gain by lis-tening to what they experienced. Yet, we find Joseph directly or indirectly offering solutions and answers to what those around him are facing.

GOD'S PRINCIPLES

While you are waiting for your own answer, God may give you the answer and solution for someone else's problem.

So the chief cupbearer told his dream to Joseph, and said to him, "In my dream, behold, there was a vine in front of me; and on the vine were three branches. And as it was budding, its blossoms came out, and its clusters produced ripe grapes. Now Pharaoh's cup was in my hand; so I took the grapes and squeezed them into Pharaoh's cup, and I put the cup into Pharaoh's hand." Then Joseph said to him, "This is the interpretation of it: the three branches are three days; within three more days Pharaoh will lift up your head and restore you to your office; and you will put Pharaoh's cup into his hand according to your former custom when you were his cupbearer. Only keep me in mind when it goes well with you, and please do me a kindness by mentioning me to Pharaoh and get me out of this house. For I was in fact kidnapped from the land of the Hebrews, and even here I have done nothing that they should have put me into the dungeon." (Genesis 40:9-14 NASB)

Joseph listens to the dream the cupbearer had and gives him an immediate interpretation. Several things can be noted about the response given by Joseph. He tells the cupbearer that in three days he will be restored to his previous position.

The second thing we can note about Joseph's response to the cupbearer is he is so certain about the interpretation of this dream and the eventual fulfillment of it that he asks for a favor. Joseph sees a glimmer of hope. He asks the cupbearer to keep him in mind when he gets his position back. Joseph further asserts his innocence in the circumstances of his life and asks the cupbearer to help get him out of prison as well.

The king's baker also had a dream. The Bible notes that when he heard that the cupbearer's dream had a positive meaning, he was ready to get his dream interpreted. The text appears to convey there may have been some anticipation of a similar meaning to his dream.

> *When the chief baker saw that he had interpreted favorably, he said to Joseph, "I also saw in my dream, and behold, there were three baskets of white bread on my head; and in the top basket there were some of all sorts of baked food for Pharaoh, and the birds were eating them out of the basket on my head." Then Joseph answered and said, "This is its interpretation: the three baskets are three days; within three more days Pharaoh will lift up your head from you and will hang you on a tree, and the birds will eat your flesh off you."* (Genesis 40:16-18 NASB)

While the cupbearer received good news, after the baker shares his dream with Joseph, Joseph gives him some bad news. He lets him know that in three days he would die. We know from what we have learned about Joseph's character, he probably didn't take any joy in delivering this news. However, integrity demanded he be honest in his conveying of the dream's interpretation.

GOD'S PRINCIPLES

**We must use any gift God gives to us
with honesty and integrity.
It is more important for our gifts
to garner respect than applause.**

Thus it came about on the third day, which was Pharaoh's birthday, that he made a feast for all his servants; and he lifted up the head of the chief cupbearer and the head of the chief baker among his servants. He restored the chief cupbearer to his office, and he put the cup into Pharaoh's hand: but he hanged the chief baker, just as Joseph had interpreted to them. Yet the chief cupbearer did not remember Joseph, but forgot him. (Genesis 40:20-23 NASB)

Have you ever reached a point in your life where you felt like it was finally your moment and after all you had been through, things were finally going to turn around for you?

GOD'S PRINCIPLES

God's vision for our lives often takes much longer than we think, and often comes to pass in a way much different than we may have planned.

This was Joseph's experience. He had cared for the cupbearer. He showed concern and compassion for him. He interpreted his dream accurately. The cupbearer was fully restored to his position. Joseph had every reason to believe this was his moment. He had already laid the groundwork. All he needed now was the cupbearer to come through on the favor he asked for and he'd finally be out of jail. "Yet the chief cupbearer did not remember Joseph, but forgot him" (Genesis 40:23 NASB).

As we close this chapter, we need to realize what really happened here. As we grasp this, we will better understand the importance of relying on God and God alone. The Bible tells us the cupbearer forgot Joseph. If we didn't dig deep into this and just left it at a surface level of understanding, what occurred would have been bad enough. The word "forget" conveys the idea of "losing the use for." This is critically powerful to understand. If we carry this to its logical conclusion, we can infer that the cupbearer returned to his position with the king and no longer had any use for Joseph who cared for him, showed him compassion, and interpreted his dream for him. From this, we will lift a few concluding principles.

GOD'S PRINCIPLES

**Never depend on a man to do what only
God can ultimately do. God is responsible for your future.**

**You may be forgotten by man,
but you will never be forgotten by God.**

**Silent appreciation is of little value.
We must never forget those who have
encouraged and helped us along the way.**

You must **never depend on a man to do what only God can ultimately do. God is responsible for your future.** There will be times in life when the people you have helped do not return the favor. There will be moments in your life, where the people you cared for no longer care about you. Do not allow these moments to make you bitter. Use these experiences to remember that **you may be forgotten by man, but you will never be forgotten by God.**

The last principle that we must glean from Joseph's experience in this chapter is that **silent appreciation is of little value. We must never forget those who have encouraged and helped us along the way.** In our current culture, there is a lack of gratitude and appreciation for those who have paved the way, cared for us, and showed compassion to us when we were at our weakest moments. Let this not be the testimony and the legacy that we choose to leave.

When you are forgotten or discarded, it can be difficult to see hope. When your expectations and dreams seem just beyond your reach, it can be easy to give up and quit. I want to challenge you with this last principle to do something we must all learn to do if we want to experience the fulfillment of all that God has for us.

GOD'S PRINCIPLES

**We must become proficient at making the most and
best of every situation, whether favorable or unfavorable.**

We can only do this with a firm belief that God remains firmly
in control of the destiny He has designed for our lives.

If you have experienced the disappointment of being forgotten,
you will find new and fresh faith from the lessons you will learn
through the rest of Joseph's experiences. In the next chapter, we
will examine the principle of preparation and lay a foundation for
studying the remainder of Joseph's life. Stay encouraged and be
prepared to observe what happens when godly preparation and
timely opportunity meet together.

Prayer

*Father, search my heart and help me to remove any bitterness
that needs to be removed for me to walk out my purpose with
freedom. Help me to forgive those who have forgotten about me.
Forgive me for any time in which there were those I could have
helped and chose not to help. Remind me daily, You are ultimately
responsible for bringing me to a place of manifestation and fulfillment of all You have promised. This day, I commit to placing
my hope and faith only in You and trust You to bring about Your
perfect and pleasing plan in my life. In Jesus' name, Amen.*

REVIEW GOD'S PRINCIPLES

Here are the important principles God has revealed to us in
that chapter.

+ **The most important factor in accomplishing anything
for God is His presence.**

+ **God's presence always produces God's favor and God's
favor leads to God's promotion.**

✦ Your circumstances can never truly imprison your purpose. Focus on your purpose and allow God to deal with your position.

✦ Use your position and authority in this world to help people.

✦ While you are waiting for your own answer, God may give you the answer and solution for someone else's problem.

✦ We must use any gift God gives to us with honesty and integrity. It is more important for our gifts to garner respect rather than applause.

✦ God's vision for our lives often takes much longer than we think and often comes to pass in a way much different than we may have planned.

✦ Never depend on a man to do what only God can ultimately do. God is responsible for your future.

✦ You may be forgotten by man, but you will never be forgotten by God.

✦ Silent appreciation is of little value. We must never forget those who have encouraged us and help us along the way.

✦ We must become proficient at making the most and best of every situation, whether favorable or unfavorable.

Reflect on how these principles encourage you on your personal journey living on the edge of destiny and how to correctly handle things when it feels like you have been forgotten.

Chapter 11

THE POWER OF PREPARATION

B efore we rejoin the life of Joseph, we want to briefly look at another godly characteristic that is needful to see God's vision fulfilled in our lives. In this chapter, we will examine the quality of preparedness. This often goes overlooked in the life of the believer. It is crucial we understand the importance of being prepared for any opportunity that God gives us. Our greatest moments may occur when our godly preparation comes face-to-face with the right opportunity or situation.

What exactly is preparation? Preparation refers to *the action or process of making something ready for use or service or of getting ready for some occasion, test, or duty.*[8] When we talk about living by faith and God's fulfillment of His vision for us, it is very easy to discount the vital role preparation plays in helping us to see success and progress in that which we do. When we look at Joseph's next phase of life in the next chapter, we will see the crucial nature of preparation played out in his life.

We notice the Bible has quite a bit to say about preparation. In Luke 14:28-30, Jesus strongly emphasizes this principle.

> *"Suppose one of you wants to build a tower. Won't you first sit down and estimate the cost to see if you have enough money to complete it? For if you lay the foundation and are not able to finish it, everyone who sees it will ridicule*

---

[8] https://www.merriam-webster.com/dictionary/preparation

you, saying, 'This person began to build and wasn't able to finish.'" (Luke 14:28-30 NIV)

The first thing we can observe is **preparation makes us ready for the opportunities God places in front of us.** Surely you can remember a time in which you could have benefited from or taken advantage positively of a situation had you been prepared for it. What good is an opportunity if you cannot capitalize on it? What benefit is an open door that we have the inability to walk through?

The second vital principle to understand regarding preparation is **it not only allows you to begin an assignment, it allows you to also see it through to completion.** We can all point to times in which we learned the hard sometimes it is easier to start something than it was to finish it. When we practice preparing ourselves, God will be able to use us mightily in many situations.

Perhaps the most applicable verse regarding preparation as it aligns with the life of Joseph is found in Proverbs 16:1, *"The preparations of the heart belong to man,* but the answer of the tongue is from the Lord" (NKJV).

The fulfillment of any godly vision or dream is the fruit of dual responsibility. God will not do what He has given us the capability to do. God will not make us try to do what only He can do. This is crucially important to understand. However, **preparation is always our responsibility.**

GOD'S PRINCIPLES

Preparation not only allows you to begin an assignment, it allows you to also see it through to completion.

The fulfillment of any godly vision or dream is the fruit of dual responsibility. Preparation is always our responsibility.

Understanding these principles is so important because the life of the believer is supernatural. We believe in the presence and power of God. We believe that the working of miracles is a great testimony to our walk with the Lord. With that said, we must understand that these things do not ever negate the need for us to be adequately prepared to do all that God has called us to do. Much of the frustration we experience and the excuse we sometimes make can ultimately be traced back to a lack of adequate and sufficient preparation.

When we consider the importance of preparation and begin to apply the principle to our lives, we will end up being more fruitful, more faithful, and more productive in our lives. When we practice preparation, we can experience the blessing of God in our families, our homes, our ministries, our jobs, and other various assignments in our lives.

Consider how many times we could have made better use of opportunities in our lives. Think about how much less stress we may experience simply through practicing preparation. When we rejoin Joseph in the next chapter of this book, we will see that he practiced preparation in simple and practical ways.

GOD'S PRINCIPLES

The fruit of preparation is promotion.

One who practices preparation understands desire will never be more important than discipline.

Preparation allows us to be prepared for every opportunity God gives us.

We cannot control when opportunities arise, but we can control our readiness to take advantage of them when they come.

As you read those principles, you probably thought of many times in your life when opportunities were more recognizable when you were prepared to seize them. You may have also noticed that things you wanted to do seemed just out of reach and the realm of possibility when you were unprepared.

What we will learn is somethings may take a long time, but if we are ready for them, we can move quickly on all God wants to do in our lives. As we look at the remainder of Joseph's life, we will see just how vital it is to take a moment to prepare.

However, preparation should never paralyze us. We can spend so much time trying to be ready, we never do what we are preparing to do. The reality is when we are prepared, God will present us with an opportunity. Our preparation, our faith, and our trust will give us the boldness and courage to move on to what He has placed in front of us.

In concluding this chapter, I want to challenge you to boldly look at the importance of preparation and view the next opportunities in your life with fresh eyes. Preparation will not only bring you to life-changing moments, but will allow you to take advantage of them.

Prayer

Father, I thank You for the gift of time to prepare. Forgive me for the moments that I missed because I was not ready. Help me to realize that preparation helps me to see the opportunities that are in front of me. Help me to walk with humility and bring me to places of promotion so that You will be glorified through my life. Like Joseph, help me to make a difference that affects generations beyond me. In Jesus' name, Amen.

Review God's Principles

Here are the important principles God has revealed to us in that chapter.

✦ **Preparation makes us ready for the opportunities God places in front of us.**

✦ **Preparation not only allows you to begin an assignment, it allows you to see it through to completion.**

✦ **The fulfillment of any godly vision or dream is the fruit of dual responsibility.**

✦ **Preparation is always our responsibility.**

✦ **The fruit of preparation is promotion. One who practices preparation understands desire will never be more important than discipline.**

✦ **We cannot control when opportunities arise, but we can control our readiness to take advantage of them when they come.**

Reflect on how these principles encourage you on your personal journey living on the edge of destiny and how to prepare for the opportunities God places before you.

Chapter 12
IT ALL MAKES SENSE NOW

We will all reach a point in our lives when it looks like the unfair and difficult experiences of our lives finally seem to make sense. This is how we might describe Joseph's life. Up to this point, Joseph has been sold by his brothers, wrongly imprisoned, and forgotten by those he has helped. While he experienced success in every circumstance and situation of his life, the favor in his life appears to yield a primary benefit to others and not necessarily to himself. The recurring theme we see played out in his life is the presence of the Lord has brought him favor, promotion, and success at whatever he does.

GOD'S PRINCIPLES

God never wastes an experience.

We will see how all of the previous experiences prepare Joseph for the promotion that will lead to his freedom and the preservation of his family.

> *Now it happened at the end of two full years that Pharaoh had a dream, and behold, he was standing by the Nile. And lo, from the Nile there came up seven cows, sleek and fat; and they grazed in the marsh grass. Then behold, seven other cows came up after them from the Nile, ugly and gaunt, and they stood by the other cows on the bank of*

the Nile. The ugly and gaunt cows ate up the seven sleek and fat cows. Then Pharaoh awoke. He fell asleep and dreamed a second time; and behold, seven ears of grain came up on a single stalk, plump and good. Then behold, seven ears, thin and scorched by the east wind, sprouted up after them. The thin ears swallowed up the seven plump and full ears. Then Pharaoh awoke, and behold, it was a dream. Now in the morning his spirit was troubled, so he sent and called for all the magicians of Egypt, and all its wise men. And Pharaoh told them his dreams, but there was no one who could interpret them to Pharaoh. (Genesis 41:1-8 NASB)

We last left Joseph forgotten in prison. He was there for two years after interpreting the dream of the cupbearer. He had every reason to believe that this is where he would remain. However, we will see Joseph is about to learn a very important principle.

GOD'S PRINCIPLES

Sometimes, the calling on our life will be revealed through the crisis in someone else's life.

In the passage above, we read that Pharaoh has two dreams that trouble him. As he begins to share his dreams, there is no one within his sphere of influence that is able to provide an interpretation. What happens next gives us a clear indication that God is always in control and that while man may forget you, God never will.

Then the chief cupbearer spoke to Pharaoh, saying, "I would make mention today of my own offenses. Pharaoh was furious with his servants, and he put me in confinement in the house of the captain of the bodyguard, both me and the chief baker. We had a dream on the same night, he and I; each of us dreamed according to the interpretation of his own dream. Now a Hebrew youth was with us there, a servant of the captain of the bodyguard, and we related them to him, and he interpreted our dreams for us. To each one he interpreted according to his own dream. And just as he interpreted for us, so it happened; he restored me in my office, but he hanged him." (Genesis 41:9-13 NASB)

Here we read the beginning of how Joseph's life is about to change. The cupbearer looks at how distraught Pharaoh is regarding the dreams and the effect the lack of an interpretation has on him. All we are told from the text is that it caused the cupbearer to remember his experience when he had a dream that could not be explained. He shares it with Pharaoh and that he knows of someone who can help.

Before we get to the main subject matter of this chapter, we can make a couple of observations. First, we can see from the text that the cupbearer had to be willing to rehash his own mistakes in order to help Pharaoh. Second, he had to be willing to acknowledge his own failure of not mentioning Joseph previously. We must consider within all of this the complete sovereignty of God. Even though Joseph appeared to have been forgotten and forsaken, a situation arises in which there is a problem that only he can serve as a bridge to answer.

Then Pharaoh sent and called for Joseph, and they hurriedly brought him out of the dungeon; and when he had shaved himself and changed his clothes, he came to Pharaoh. Pharaoh said to Joseph, "I have had a dream, but no one can interpret it; and I have heard it said about you, that when you hear a dream you can interpret it." (Genesis 41:14-15 NASB)

GOD'S PRINCIPLES

**We need not worry about missing our moment.
We must only concern ourselves with being prepared
for our moment when it arrives.**

In looking at the passage, we can see a couple of critical things. Pharaoh hears about Joseph and sends for him, but we can easily miss a small but significant detail. Joseph shaves and changes his clothes prior to going to meet Pharaoh. We have no indication as to whether Joseph was told why Pharaoh wanted to meet with him at the time. We only know that Pharaoh called and Joseph prepared himself for the meeting.

As Joseph comes to Pharaoh, no time is wasted in laying out the reasons for the meeting. When we read the Bible, sometimes it is easy for us to overlook the truth of human tendencies and conditions. When Joseph is presented with Pharaoh's greeting, it would have been easy for him to approach it pridefully. After all, Joseph has had previous experience with dreams and the interpretation of the same. However, we find Joseph approaches Pharaoh with both faith and humility.

*Joseph then answered Pharaoh, saying, "It is not in me; God will give Pharaoh a favorable answer." (*Genesis 41:16 NASB)

Joseph expresses to Pharaoh that what he is looking for will not come from Joseph, but from God. In other words, Joseph presents God as the answer to Pharaoh's problem.

GOD'S PRINCIPLES

What God chooses to do through us is not about us but about Him.

The collective experiences of Joseph's life have taught him to focus the attention on God and not himself. Because he does this, he can speak with certainty about God's ability and willingness to provide Pharaoh with an answer. After the aforementioned exchange, Pharaoh chooses to relay his dreams to Joseph.

Now Joseph said to Pharaoh, "Pharaoh's dreams are one and the same; God has told to Pharaoh what He is about to do. The seven good cows are seven years; and the seven good ears are seven years; they are one and the same dream. The seven lean and ugly cows that came up after them are seven years, and the seven thin ears scorched by the east wind will be seven years of famine. It is as I have spoken to Pharaoh: God has shown to Pharaoh what He is about to do. Behold, seven years of great abundance are coming in all the land of Egypt; and after them seven years of famine will come, and all the abundance will be forgotten in the land of Egypt, and the famine will ravage the land. So the abundance will be unknown in the land because of that subsequent famine; for it will be very severe. Now as for the repeating of the dream to Pharaoh twice, it means that the matter is determined by God, and God will quickly bring it about. Now let Pharaoh look for a man discerning and wise, and set him over the land of Egypt. Let Pharaoh take action to appoint overseers in charge of the land, and let him exact a fifth of the produce of the land of Egypt in the seven years of abundance. Then let them gather all the food of these good years that are coming, and store up the grain for food in the cities under Pharaoh's authority, and let them guard it. Let the food become as a reserve for the land for the seven years of famine which will occur in the land of Egypt, so that the land will not perish during the famine." (Genesis 41:25-36 NASB)

The passage above shows us first, Joseph interprets the dream. Note, this is all that Joseph was brought into Pharaoh's presence to do, but it is not all that he does.

GOD'S PRINCIPLES

When given a task, always do more than is expected of you.

Joseph explained that the land will experience seven prosperous years and seven years of famine. He shares that the famine will be so severe that people will forget the prosperous time. If he would have stopped at this, he would have done what he was summoned to do. The interesting thing to note is that he not only shares what will happen, but he also provides Pharaoh with a wise plan to address the years of plenty and the years of famine. He even suggests that Pharaoh put someone in charge of it.

The next observation we can infer from the response of Joseph is that he was **not** a self-promoter. He remains unconcerned with trying to secure any type of position for himself. He is only concerned with doing what he was asked to do by God. God would now use the response of Pharaoh to change Joseph's life forever.

> *Joseph's suggestions were well received by Pharaoh and his officials. So Pharaoh asked his officials, "Can we find anyone else like this man so obviously filled with the spirit of God?" Then Pharaoh said to Joseph, "Since God has revealed the meaning of the dreams to you, clearly no one else is as intelligent or wise as you are. You will be in charge of my court, and all my people will take orders from you. Only I, sitting on my throne, will have a rank higher than yours."* (Genesis 41:37-40 NLT)

Because Joseph was able to interpret Pharaoh's dream and provide wise counsel as to how to move forward, he receives a promotion. It must be noted that this promotion is much different than when he was promoted in the house of Potiphar and when he was promoted in the prison. Now, we see a promotion where Joseph receives exponential influence and authority in a moment. He goes from being a prisoner to being in charge of the entire land and second only to Pharaoh. Look at how Pharaoh describes Joseph's new assignment.

> *Pharaoh said to Joseph, "I hereby put you in charge of the entire land of Egypt." Then Pharaoh removed his signet ring from his hand and placed it on Joseph's finger. He dressed him in fine linen clothing and hung a gold chain around his neck. Then he had Joseph ride in the chariot reserved for his second-in-command. And*

wherever Joseph went, the command was shouted, "Kneel down!" So Pharaoh put Joseph in charge of all Egypt. And Pharaoh said to him, "I am Pharaoh, but no one will lift a hand or foot in the entire land of Egypt without your approval." (Genesis 41:41-44 NLT)

As we close this chapter, we can find encouragement in several things. We can see our lives can change in a moment.

GOD'S PRINCIPLES

We are never truly slaves to our circumstances when we serve a God who can show us favor.

Our present situation is never truly final.

God can always shift us from where we are to where He desires for us to be.

God may use a crisis in somebody else's life to reveal the purpose in your life.

When God brings us to problem junctures in the lives of others, it is quite possible He will use us to reveal the solution.

What should we do with what we have observed in this chapter? I want to encourage you not to despise the place you are currently in. It is possible that your current situation is merely a set-up for your promotion. You must be willing to use unpleasant times to prepare you for your moment.

GOD'S PRINCIPLES

If we are distracted by our distresses, we will miss opportunities to grow and mature.

In short, when we have a relationship with God, we must be willing to make the most of where we are while believing God will take us to the place He desires for us to be.

In the next chapter, we will see how Joseph handles his position of leadership and the various important principles that we can personally draw from what he experienced.

Prayer

Father, thank You for my present circumstances. Whether I have chosen my present situation or not, I know You are with me. Help me to make the most where I am while You help me to prepare for where You are taking me. I forgive those who have forgotten me. I forgive myself for those I have forgotten. Give me the wisdom to do what You have called me to do. Give me understanding and humility so that my actions reflect Your glory. Never allow me to be tempted to present myself as the answer rather than You. Thank You in advance for Your favor and promotion, in Jesus' name, Amen.

REVIEW GOD'S PRINCIPLES

Here are the important principles God has revealed to us in that chapter.

+ **God never wastes an experience.**

+ **Sometimes, the calling on our life will be revealed through the crisis in someone else's life.**

+ **We need not worry about missing our moment. We must only concern ourselves with being prepared for our moment when it arrives.**

+ **What God chooses to do through us is not about us but about Him.**

✦ When given a task, always do more than is expected of you.

✦ We are never truly slaves to our circumstances when we serve a God who can show us favor.

✦ Our present situation is never truly final. God can always shift us from where we are to where He desires for us to be.

✦ God may use a crisis in somebody else's life to reveal the purpose in your life.

✦ When God brings us to problem junctures in the lives of others, it is quite possible that He will use us to reveal the solution.

✦ If we are distracted by our distresses, we will miss opportunities to grow and mature.

Reflect on how these principles encourage you on your personal journey living on the edge of destiny and how to correctly handle your experiences along the way.

Chapter 13

THE WEALTH OF WISDOM

As we near the conclusion of our discussion on the life of Joseph, we need to discuss the next qualities that we see played out in his life. Within this chapter and the next, we address two qualities that prove the character of Joseph in his journey to godly promotion. We will also explore how these qualities are important to our lives.

In this chapter, we will look at the importance of wisdom. In the next chapter, we will address the necessity of practicing forgiveness. We will then return to the life of Joseph and see how these two qualities make all the difference in how we handle positions of power and authority in our lives.

Wisdom is perhaps one of the most needful tools to fully live out the plans and the purpose God has for our lives. Proverbs 4:7 says, *"The beginning of wisdom is this: Get wisdom. Though it cost all you have, get understanding."* What we can observe from this passage of Scripture is that the acquisition of godly wisdom must become a priority in our lives.

Secondly, wisdom may have a cost. We must be willing to pay the price to get the wisdom that we need to fulfill the purpose and plan that God has for our lives. It is important to remember this cost is not always monetary. Sometimes, as we have seen with the life of Joseph, that price is experience. At other times, that price is the challenge we are called to overcome.

GOD'S PRINCIPLES

**Since wisdom is a priority, never waste a test.
Utilize your tests to help you gain the wisdom
that will help you in the next season of your life.**

The next thing that is important to realize about *true wisdom* is that it only comes from God. Proverbs 2:6 says, *"For the LORD gives wisdom; from his mouth come knowledge and understanding."* *True wisdom* is discovered in His Word. It is found in His ways, His principles, and His patterns. It is absolutely necessary for us to seek God and depend on Him to receive the wisdom we need to navigate the situations of our lives in a way that will bring Him glory and help us to function properly as we fulfill His assignment for our life.

James 3:17 says, *"But the wisdom that comes from heaven is first of all pure; then peace-loving, considerate, submissive, full of mercy and good fruit, impartial and sincere."* James reveals that godly wisdom is such that it produces good fruit in our lives. When we possess godly wisdom, we are not using it to gain an advantage or come off better than anybody else.

GOD'S PRINCIPLES

**Godly wisdom always produces good fruit.
Where you find wisdom, you will find fruitfulness.**

If we understand this, we realize the necessity of being fully aware of what godly wisdom actually is. Wisdom is defined as *the capacity to understand and so have skill in living.*[9] This definition has serious implications for our lives. It means that in order to live properly, we must have an understanding of what is happening and the skill to use that understanding to live in a way that pleases God. If we realize this, we can begin to see that many situations in our lives may be easier to deal with when we become proficient at gaining and applying godly wisdom. We will see this when we return to the life of Joseph.

---

[9] https://www.merriam-webster.com/dictionary/wisdom

In considering all that we have stated already, we must then ask a very important question. If wisdom is needed in our lives and it comes from God, how can we get it? James 1:5-8 gives us a clear answer.

> *But if any of you lacks wisdom, let him ask of God, who gives to all generously and without reproach, and it will be given to him. But he must ask in faith without any doubting, for the one who doubts is like the surf of the sea, driven and tossed by the wind. For that man ought not to expect that he will receive anything from the Lord, being a double-minded man, unstable in all his ways. (NASB)*

God gives us the recipe for walking in wisdom.

➤ **Step 1:** We must ask God for it. This may seem like a simple point, but if God has it, that is who we need to ask for it.

➤ **Step 2:** We must realize God is willing to give us wisdom. He does not point out our faults or show partiality in pouring out wisdom into our lives.

➤ **Step 3:** We must ask for godly wisdom in faith, believing that He will provide the wisdom that we are requesting.

➤ **Step 4:** We must not doubt because if we are doubtful, we will be hesitant and timid in applying the wisdom God wants to give us.

When we return to the conclusion of Joseph's life in Chapter 15, we will see that Joseph unashamedly applied godly wisdom to the situations he was given. The wisdom Joseph applied to his life led to his promotion and to his ability to function in his calling and assignment in a way that blessed and benefited the people whom he was called to serve.

As we gain more clarity into our personal calling and assignment for our lives, we will appreciate God pouring out all the knowledge and understanding that we need. Imagine the satisfaction and fulfillment of knowing God will use us to live in a way that provides blessing far beyond our wildest dreams.

Prayer

Father, I know that all wisdom ultimately resides with You. I realize that wisdom must become a priority in my life in order to function properly in the calling and assignment You have for me. I ask You for Your wisdom in faith, believing You have the ability to provide it without finding fault in me. In Jesus' name, Amen.

REVIEW GOD'S PRINCIPLES

Here are the important principles God has revealed to us in that chapter.

✦ **Since wisdom is a priority, never waste a test.**

✦ **Utilize your tests to help you gain the wisdom that will help in the next season of your life.**

✦ **Godly wisdom always produces good fruit.**

✦ **Where you find wisdom, you will find fruitfulness.**

Reflect on how these principles encourage you on your personal journey living on the edge of destiny and how to receive the godly wisdom you will need to complete your assignment from God.

Ask Yourself...
Am I willing to walk in wisdom?
Am I willing to ask God to provide me with the very wisdom I need?

Chapter 14

THE POWER OF FORGIVENESS

As we near the last part of this book, we want to briefly look at the last and perhaps one of the most crucial qualities for fulfilling the assignment God has on our lives. One of the things that happen in our lives as we near our destiny moments is the appearance of where we need to demonstrate and practice forgiveness. As we become aware of areas in which we need to show forgiveness to others, we can observe these can easily become crossroad moments in our lives. What we do when we meet these moments will show us whether we have developed everything we need to live out fully the destiny calling God has for our lives. Let us look briefly at what the Bible has to say about forgiveness.

GOD'S PRINCIPLES

**Forgiveness is not a matter of the head,
but a matter of the heart.**

The first thing we must understand is **forgiveness is not a matter of the head, but a matter of the heart.** Ephesians 4:32 says, "Be kind to one another, tenderhearted, forgiving one another, as God in Christ forgave you" (ESV). Here we can see a tenderness of heart is necessary for us to practice forgiveness.

Forgiveness may be defined as *allowing room for weakness or error.*[10] One might even say that to forgive is to release someone from their debt or obligation for wrongs they have done. In all of our lives, we will have moments in which it will be crucial for us to forgive people for the errors they have committed or the weaknesses they have shown as well as the way they have affected us.

The second thing we must realize about forgiveness is that our willingness to demonstrate it will have an impact on our personal prayer life. In Mark 11:25, Jesus says, *"And whenever you stand praying, forgive, if you have anything against anyone, so that your Father also who is in heaven may forgive you your trespasses"* (ESV). Jesus shares that when we are praying, it is important to examine the relationships in our lives and be intentional about realizing if we have anything against anyone. If we do, we need to forgive them.

We have to understand we must practice forgiveness in the same way God practices forgiveness toward us. We must understand that people may wrong us, but we have also committed wrongs, made mistakes, and have personal weaknesses as well. In light of that, we must be willing to forgive others.

Therefore, confess your sins to one another and pray for one another, that you may be healed. The prayer of a righteous person has great power as it is working. (James 5:16 ESV)

We see here that the power of forgiveness is often demonstrated further in the mutual confession of faults and weaknesses within the Christian community. This is powerful because it gives fuel to our prayer life and provides an avenue of continual cleansing and healing among those who are connected to one another.

When we deal with areas of personal forgiveness in our own lives, the question may arise as to how much people can do to us before we no longer have a responsibility and obligation to forgive. After all, if people don't change, why should we forgive them?

---

[10] https://www.merriam-webster.com/dictionary/forgiveness

Then Peter came up and said to him, "Lord, how often will my brother sin against me, and I forgive him? As many as seven times?" Jesus said to him, "I do not say to you seven times, but seventy times seven." (Matthew 18:21-22 ESV)

GOD'S PRINCIPLES

**Forgiveness is unlimited.
Just as God provides unlimited forgiveness to us,
we must extend the same to others.**

Practicing forgiveness does **not** mean we provide unlimited access for people into our lives. We must still ask for wisdom concerning those we come into contact with and allow access to us. We are not under obligation to just keep leaving ourselves completely open to people to wound and injure us. With that said, we must realize that as we free people from the errors they had committed against us, we will also free ourselves from being hindered by holding any bitterness in our hearts that will keep us from fulfilling the call God has upon our lives.

Forgiveness is a part of our life. Whether we want to admit it or not, it helps us to navigate through the relationships in our lives.

GOD'S PRINCIPLES

If we are going to live in any form of community in our lives, the practice of forgiveness will be a necessity.

Colossians 3:13 says, *"Bearing with one another and, if one has a complaint against another, forgiving each other; **as the Lord has forgiven you, so you also must forgive"*** (ESV emphasis added). The point of this verse cannot be overstated. There will be times in which we will have to bear with one another. There will be many moments in which we are going to have opportunities to show patience for others as they work through errors and weaknesses. It is important to note we always practice forgiveness in the light of the truth that we all require constant forgiveness for ourselves as well.

In the last chapter of this book, we will look at the final part of Joseph's life. We will see how he demonstrates both wisdom and forgiveness in a way that shows he has developed godly character and maturity over the course of his life.

Before we proceed to this place in Joseph's life, search your heart and mind and ask God to reveal any areas of your life in which you need to demonstrate and practice forgiveness in a tangible fashion.

Prayer

Father, thank You for forgiving me. Help me now to become fully aware of any places and areas in my life in which I must demonstrate and practice forgiveness for others. You look at the errors and weaknesses in my life and You continually extend forgiveness to me. As such, I ask You to give me the capacity to empathize with and forgive others. Thank You for the truth of forgiveness as revealed in Your Word. I believe that as I forgive, my prayer life will not be hindered and I will experience fresh faith, fresh hope, and fresh courage, in Jesus' name, Amen.

REVIEW GOD'S PRINCIPLES

Here are the important principles God has revealed to us in that chapter.

+ **Forgiveness is not a matter of the head, but a matter of the heart.**

+ **Forgiveness is unlimited. Just as God provides unlimited forgiveness to us, we must extend the same to others.**

+ **If we are going to live in any form of community in our lives, the practice of forgiveness will be a necessity.**

Reflect on how these principles encourage you on your personal journey living on the edge of destiny and extending forgiveness so you can complete your assignment from God.

Ask Yourself...
Did God reveal any areas of my life in which I need to demonstrate and practice forgiveness in a tangible fashion?

List them here and be obedient to God to forgive as He has forgiven you:

_____

_____

_____

_____

Chapter 15

AN INSTRUMENT
IN GOD'S HANDS

A s we examine the final stage of Joseph's journey, we will discover several characteristics that he developed in his life that allowed him to fully walk out the assignment God planned for his life. We will also see how these very qualities are needful for us to fulfill in proper order our calling and assignment from God. We will pick up the remainder of this journey in Genesis 42.

As we return to the story, the famine predicted by Joseph is occurring and had reached the land of Canaan.

> *Now Jacob saw that there was grain in Egypt, and Jacob said to his sons, "Why are you staring at one another?" He said, "Behold, I have heard that there is grain in Egypt; go down there and buy some for us from that place, so that we may live and not die." Then ten brothers of Joseph went down to buy grain from Egypt. But Jacob did not send Joseph's brother Benjamin with his brothers, for he said, "I am afraid that harm may befall him." So the sons of Israel came to buy grain among those who were coming, for the famine was in the land of Canaan also.* (Genesis 42:1-5 NASB)

It is at this point we are going to see Joseph's life, dreams, and assignment all come full circle. We are about to observe the reunion of Joseph and the very brothers that sold him into slavery. When we read the Bible, it can be clearly observed that we are given the gift of hindsight. We see the finished story. We see that everything has worked out. The challenge with this is that we often divorce the story from the very real feelings that are occurring on the inside of those involved. Genesis 42:6-7 gives us a glimpse of what happens when Joseph is first reunited with his brothers.

Now Joseph was the ruler over the land; he was the one who sold to all the people of the land. And Joseph's brothers came and bowed down to him with their faces to the ground. When Joseph saw his brothers he recognized them, but he disguised himself to them and spoke to them harshly. And he said to them, "Where have you come from?" And they said, "From the land of Canaan, to buy food." (NASB)

As we pick up the story, we find that Joseph is in charge of providing food to all in Egypt. His brothers have come and bowed before him looking for food. The interesting thing is the text tells us Joseph recognized his brothers, but his brothers did not recognize him.

GOD'S PRINCIPLES

When we have been treated badly, we often remember those who harmed or offended us more than they do.

We don't fully know what was going through Joseph's mind. We only know that he made sure not to reveal himself to his brothers, yet. He began almost toying with them and talking to them harshly and questioning their reason for appearing in front of him.

As we continue in the text, we begin to see and further digest what was occurring and how Joseph is processing and dealing with it.

But Joseph had recognized his brothers, although they did not recognize him. Joseph remembered the dreams which he had about them, and said to them, "You are spies; you have come to look at the undefended parts of our land." Then they said to him, "No, my lord, but your servants have come to buy food. We are all sons of one man; we are honest men, your servants are not spies." Yet he said to them, "No, but you have come to look at the undefended parts of our land!" But they said, "Your servants are twelve brothers in all, the sons of one man in the land of Canaan; and behold, the youngest is with our father today, and one is no longer alive." Joseph said to them, "It is as I said to you, you are spies; by this you will be tested: by the life of Pharaoh, you shall not go from this place unless your youngest brother comes here! Send one of you that he may get your brother, while you remain confined, that your words may be tested, whether there is truth in you. But if not, by the life of Pharaoh, surely you are spies." So he put them all together in prison for three days. (Genesis 42:8-17 NASB)

When Joseph encounters his brothers as they are at a point of great need, he begins to remember the dreams he had as a teenager. Was he wrestling with revenge? Was he thinking this is now my moment to be in control? These are all reasonable things to assume and none of us might have even remotely thought any differently had we been placed in the same situation.

Essentially, the first thing Joseph does is accuses them of being spies. He questions their motives. One of the things that often troubled me about this text is that his brothers did not recognize him. I believe even though Joseph was now in a place of power and promotion, there was a part of him that had to wonder how his brothers could not have recognized him and remembered what they had done to him.

GOD'S PRINCIPLES

**One of the greatest marks of maturity
is learning to forgive others without an apology.**

At this point, Joseph puts them in prison and tells them the only way they will get food and be proven not to be spies is for their youngest brother to be brought to him.

Now Joseph said to them on the third day, "Do this and live, for I fear God: if you are honest men, let one of your brothers be confined in our prison; but as for the rest of you, go, carry grain for the famine of your households, and bring your youngest brother to me, so your words may be verified, and you will not die." And they did so. Then they said to one another, "Truly we are guilty concerning our brother, because we saw the distress of his soul when he pleaded with us, yet we would not listen; therefore this distress has come upon us." Reuben answered them, saying, "Did I not tell you, 'Do not sin against the boy'; and you would not listen? Now comes the reckoning for his blood." They did not know, however, that Joseph understood, for there was an interpreter between them. He turned away from them and wept. But when he returned to them and spoke to them, he took Simeon from them and bound him before their eyes." (Genesis 42:18-24 NASB)

This part of the story is interesting because Joseph begins to show mercy to his brothers. The unique issue with the mercy demonstrated is it finally requires his brothers to acknowledge the wrongs they committed against Joseph. In essence, Joseph says he will allow his brothers to leave and take provisions to the rest of the family, but one of the brothers must remain with him and they must come back with their youngest brother.

At this point, they both acknowledge and argue with each other about their past sins without realizing Joseph could understand what they were saying. Something about their conversation causes

Joseph to weep and feel in his heart the emotions that he had been bottled up for years. When He returns to the conversation, he proceeds to have one of His brothers detained and allows the rest of them to leave.

After Joseph's family returns, Jospeh makes provision for His family. Jospeh demonstrates high levels of understanding and forgiveness by providing the family which betrayed him with both food and shelter. There is an aspect of Joseph's maturity reflected in the fact that He is is able to see the greater purpose of God in his own struggles. Even though his brothers damaged him greatly; Joseph was able to see that God could use his experience for a higher good and make Him an instrument of deliverance in the lives of his family.

REVIEW GOD'S PRINCIPLES

Here are the important principles God has revealed to us in that chapter.

- ✦ **When we have been treated badly, we often remember those who harmed us or offended us more than they do.**

- ✦ **One of the greatest marks of maturity is learning to forgive others without an apology.**

Reflect on how these principles encourage you on your personal journey living on the edge of destiny and completing your assignment from God.

Conclusion

FAITH, FAMINE, AND FORGIVENESS

GOD'S PRINCIPLES

**Our character and maturity are revealed
by how we handle promotion and position.**

*Then Joseph said to his brothers, "Please come closer to me." And they came [closer]. And he said, "I am your brother Joseph, whom you sold into Egypt. Now **do not be grieved or angry with yourselves,** because you sold me here, for **God sent me before you to preserve life.** For the famine has been in the land these two years, and there are still five years in which there will be neither plowing nor harvesting. **God sent me before you to preserve for you a remnant in the earth,** and to **keep you alive by a great deliverance.** Now, therefore, **it was not you who sent me here, but God;** and He has made me a father to Pharaoh and lord of all his household and ruler over all the land of Egypt."* (Genesis 45:4-8 NASB emphasis added)

GOD'S PRINCIPLES

God's plan is always bigger than our limited perspective.

**We can kick people when they are down,
or we can offer them a hand up.**

God is in control.

Our detours cannot derail our assignment.

**God will not promote the partial.
He needs to determine if I can be trusted
to be a blessing to the people who did me wrong.**

When Joseph's brothers saw that their father was dead, they said, "What if Joseph bears a grudge against us and pays us back in full for all the wrong which we did to him!" So they sent a message to Joseph, saying, "Your father charged before he died, saying, 'Thus you shall say to Joseph, "Please forgive, I beg you, the transgression of your brothers and their sin, for they did you wrong."' And now, please forgive the transgression of the servants of the God of your father." And Joseph wept when they spoke to him. Then his brothers also came and fell down before him and said, "Behold, we are your servants." But **Joseph said to them, "Do not be afraid, for am I in God's place? As for you, you meant evil against me, but God meant it for good in order to bring about [this present result, to preserve many people alive.** *So therefore, do not be afraid; I will provide for you and your little ones." So he comforted them and spoke kindly to them"* (Genesis 50:15-21 NASB emphasis added)

GOD'S PRINCIPLES

**God will use what seems strange to us
to bring about His intended result.**

**If we ever want to be used by God, we will have to surrender
not only our lives, but our perspectives and perceptions.**

ABOUT THE AUTHOR

D r. Shanon Eaton, along with his wife Jessica, are the Lead Pastors of Life City Church in Jacksonville, Florida. After serving in different ministries, they felt the call to start a life-giving church in Jacksonville, Fl. Pastor Shanon earned a Bachelor's degree in Education from Clearwater Christian College and holds a Master's degree in Educational Leadership from Nova Southeastern University. He completed his education by earning a Master of Divinity degree in Evangelism and Church Growth from Liberty University. He also Holds a Doctor of Ministry Degree from Southwest Bible College & Seminary as well as an Honorary Doctor of Divinity Degree from Grace Valley Theological Seminary.

Jessica Eaton was a basketball coach, a speaker in Juvenile Detention Centers, and a Youth and Children's Pastor. Jessica has always had a passion for the next generation. Due to circumstances growing up, her faith in God was nonexistent. When Jessica was seventeen, she desired to go into the military. After discovering she was pregnant, she chose to have an abortion. She then found the Lord at the age of seventeen and hasn't turned back. God's grace and mercy on her life were so impactful and she prays God will continue to use her to share of His goodness and restoration.

CPSIA information can be obtained
at www.ICGtesting.com
Printed in the USA
LVHW011017180621
690568LV00010B/1013